LOOKING FO

The Modern Prospector's Handbook

LOOKING FOR GOLD:
The Modern Prospector's Handbook

By Bradford Angier

Illustrations by Vena Angier; U.S. Geological Survey *Principal Gold-Producing Districts of the United States*, by the late A. H. Koschmann and by M. H. Bergendahl, U.S. Geological Survey Professional Paper 610, U.S. Bureau of Mines; Nevada State Bureau of Mines; U.S. Department of the Interior; and Alaska Division of Mines and Geology.

Stackpole Books

DEDICATION

For Jeanne-Nicole Ledoux
of Expeditions Unlimited, Ltd.
who has helped

Library of Congress Cataloging in Publication Data

Angier, Bradford.
  Looking for gold.

  1. Prospecting.   2. Gold.   I. Title
TN271.G6A53   622'.18'41   74-23258
ISBN 0-8117-2034-9

CONTENTS

Chapter One

NUGGETS ARE IN

THE BEST TIME to be anywhere in this continent's widespread if often unrecognized gold-enriched areas is now. Opportunity and optimism have increased along with the opening of new hard-asset frontiers. There's a boom-time beat. Newcomers are finding they can have a piece of this action, where in more structured and less individualized occupations they might be excluded. They're loving every moment.

In 1934, the governments of the world fixed gold's price at $35 an ounce to settle international payments. To keep the price there, they began to sell their own reserves. When dangerously emptying treasuries made it evident in 1968 that they could no longer support this artificial level, the two-tier system was established.

The price of the monetary gold used among nations for paying debts was pegged at a set figure, which was $42.22 in the spring of 1980. On the free market, gold was permitted to float. One of the more cautious analysts looked "for significantly higher prices over the long term." The trend can go either way, but the rumor was "$1,500 an ounce."

One reason, along with the general flight from paper currencies and the Middle East uncertainty, is the cost of a barrel of OPEC oil. Since the forties, the Arab petroleum-producing countries that dominate world markets have proceeded by the rule of thumb that one ounce of gold equals roughly fifteen barrels of their oil. The cartel uneasiness about the role of the U. S. dollar in international oil trade was increased by this country's freeze of Iranian assets after the takeover of the American embassy and by the fact that OPEC's current account surplus was projected to reach $115 billion by the end of 1980.

Although some people buy gold to make money, others accumulate it to keep what money they have. In 1975, private ownership of gold bullion became legal in the United States for the first time since 1933 in the F. D. Roosevelt era. However, millions of individuals in Europe and elsewhere, have been adding to their personal hoards for years and watching them maintain their values despite unstable currencies, kiting prices, devaluation, deficit financing, devastating inflation, civil rebellion, and even war. Historically, gold has been a refuge for people nervous about their money. With the world's paper money in still another inflationary spiral, gold now represents for many a haven.

Adventurers in other centuries discovered new worlds in their search for this enduringly precious and essentially indestructible element. In ancient days, gold was considered the emblem of eternal life. Throughout the ages it has been a sign of stature, wealth, and power—ever bright, scarce, malleable, noncorrosive, never tarnishing, compact, enticing, and the one traditional possession that can be objectively evaluated.

In North America where Canada, the world's third largest producer, is now symbolically minting the one-ounce, 99.9 percent pure, legal tender coin, the Maple Leaf, the searching by weekend and full-time prospectors goes on with increasing success. In this country, panners and dredgers on Colorado's upper Rio Grande River have recovered thousands of ounces in recent years, while so-called hippies have taken vegetable cans of gold out of other watercourses in the state. Just below, in New Mexico, gold has been found in all the counties along the Rio Grande and the Colorado line. Dry placers on both sides of the Colorado River in Arizona have been profitably worked during the same period with dry concentrates and vibrators. Gold dredges are now being operated in Indiana's Brown and surrounding counties and east and south of Asheville in North Carolina. In New England, too, Spartan dredges with their tapered sluice boxes are evident.

Beach placering is taking over in parts of the hemisphere; dredgers work up the rivers one hundred yards to one-quarter mile from their mouths to get the yellow metal in banks and stream beds that dropped out when the flow met high tide.

Some dry lakes and ponds inland are also giving up rich pockets in areas where runoffs or arroyos drain. Although this usually means working dust, which can be very dirty, when part is gold dust the rest doesn't seem to matter.

In certain regions, hydraulic rams elevate water to the camp or operating location, sometimes providing the right amount for a one or two-man rocker, trammel, or sluice. Not needing artificial power, Long Toms are sometimes used in clandestine placers to avoid the racket of engines.

"Many miners do not report their activities nor their production due to fear of official meddling in their activities, even though perfectly legal," notes Dean Miller, editor of *National Prospector's Gazette & Treasure Hunter's News,* which dates back to the late 1800s. "Some laws and edicts cause more time to be spent with applications, red tape, and inspectors than in operating, so miners simply operate and ignore the rest."

Thomas B. Nolan, head of the U. S. Geological Survey, said a few years ago that ten times as many mining regions may remain to be found in this country as are already known, and, furthermore, that these should include as many primary areas as there are now. Despite all the prospecting of the past, vast districts, even readily accessible ones, have scarcely been touched. How much chance does the amateur and the weekend prospector still have? More than 80 percent of the major finds of uranium and other radioactive ores in recent years have been made by inexperienced prospectors.

Not so long ago in Australia, where the Western Mining Corporation had a pair of professional geology teams working in the region, a lone prospector by the name of Kenneth Shirley uncovered the rich Poseidon mine. John Jones, a young prospector cruising over a district carefully covered by experienced geologists, became a millionaire by finding the Scotia nickel deposit.

Up in the already thickly staked Klondike a latecomer from California, Al Lancaster, found some white gravel on a high bench which proved to be part of an old riverbed. While others laughed at him, for the heavy metal was supposed to have been deposited low down, he staked the first bench claim in that part of the Yukon and produced $200,000 in gold.

Luck sometimes runs in streaks. Clarence Berry sluiced $1½ million from his diggings in the Klondike, whereupon he moved with his brothers to Fairbanks where on Esther Creek they found a bonanza for a second time. After this, they went back to California, invested in oil lands around Bakersfield, and made a third fortune. In more recent years a college lad scooped up some $70,000 in gold nuggets during an Alaskan summer, which capitalized him to drill for Kansas oil, which furnished the wherewithal for substantial Colorado land investments.

There's always Lady Luck. Harry Preston, prospecting in Ontario, slipped on a hillside near Porcupine Lake, scraping the moss from a quartz ledge that he and his two compansions followed to a dome-shaped formation that was yellow with gold and which became the world-famous Dome mine. Up to now, the Porcupine gold district has produced more than $1½ billion.

Nor was gold the only precious metal produced in that Province by chance. Fred LaRose, a blacksmith employed by an Ontario railroad, heaved his hammer at a skulking fox, missed the animal, and broke off a hunk of rock to uncover a bright vein of silver which became the rich LaRose mine.

Bennie Hollinger, a young barber so broke that he was getting along on a $45 grubstake from Jack McMahon who immediately sold a half interest in his prospects to Gilbert Labine for $55, was one of the prospectors who invaded the Porcupine area following the Preston find. He yanked some moss off some rocks and found a vein of quartz that looked as if hot taffy had become intermingled with freezing snow. Thus was the beginning of the fabulous Hollinger mine, one of this continent's richest gold producers.

Earlier in the Sacramento Valley of California one frosty January morning in 1848 an itinerant carpenter who was putting up a sawmill on the South Fork of the American River for Johann Augustus Sutter saw something gleaming in the bottom of the new millrace, picked it up, found another, and exclaimed to his fellow workers, "Boys, I think I have found a gold mine."

By the end of that year no less than $6 million in the yellow metal had been won by the early stampeders. During the first four years after James Marshall's discovery, California gold diggings produced more than $220 million. Between the second year after the find and 1900, gold production in California never dropped below $11,200,000 a year.

So rich was the area around Downieville, California, that a prospector, Al Callis, discovered gold one Sunday morning merely by kicking at the ground with his foot. Callis, who was a religious man, covered the strike over until Monday when he could work the new find with a clear conscience.

George Carmack and two Indians, Tagish Charlie and Skookum Jim, were on the Klondike River in northwestern Canada, looking for logs to float downriver to sell at a Fortymile mill for $25 a thousand feet. There is some dispute as to exactly what happened, but one story is that Skookum Jim, having killed a moose for camp meat, was washing a dish pan in Rabbit Creek when he saw gold lying between the flaking rock in the stream bed. All three staked claims on what was renamed Bonanza Creek, and the Klondike gold stampede was on.

Another barber, this one Uly Gaisford from Tacoma, thought so little of the claim he staked on the Creek that he moved along to Circle City to resume work with his scissors and was later astonished when his land brought in $50,000 inside a year.

All Bonanza Creek had been staked by the latter part of August. Down the stream tramped Antone Stander, a young immigrant who had arrived from Austria, unable to speak English, with less than two dollars and who was now hungry and nearly destitute. On an impulse he and three companions, each also near the end of his resources, staked on the narrow wooded south fork of the Creek.

One was Frank Keller who'd been a California railway brakeman. Another, Frank Phiscator, was a Michigan farm boy who had worked his way west. The fourth, Jay Whipple, was an old gravel puncher who'd strayed down from the Sixtymile area. Later called Eldorado Creek, this fork proved to be the richest stream in the world, each of the quartet of claims that were staked that day finally producing $1 million or more apiece.

Some Scotsmen from Nanaimo on British Columbia's Vancouver Island staked Claims 14, 15, 16, and 17 on this still unproved Eldorado Creek for which the experienced prospectors on hand had little regard. The Scotsmen later gave up the last two in order to keep rights on another brook, which turned out to amount to little. Tom Lippy, because his wife wanted a log cabin, left his claim higher on Eldorado Creek to move into the timber and so restaked No. 16 for himself. There proved to be only a small amount of gold on the upper Eldorado, but No. 16 brought Lippy and his home-loving wife over $1½ million.

Charlie Anderson, drunk, bought a claim on Eldorado for $800, was unable to get his money back when he sobered up, and dourly took off for the claim where $1 million in gold awaited him in the bedrock. In fact, although the sourdoughs said that the geography of Eldorado

Creek, so named as a joke, was all wrong, almost every claim from one to 40 turned out to be worth at least half a million dollars. And this was at the turn of the century when a square meal cost a quarter, a quart of whiskey less than twice that, coffee sold for fourteen cents a pound, a basket of fresh tomatoes three cents, an all-wool suit went for four dollars, and a four-room apartment might be rented for six dollars a month.

A wrong measurement on Bonanza Creek left open a slab of land 86 feet broad at its widest spot. Dick Lowe, a chain man on a survey crew, decided to stake it after failing to find a larger fraction. He had no luck in selling it for $900 or even leasing it, so he dug a shaft himself. Nothing! He tried again, and this time washed out $46,000 in eight hours. The tiny pie-shaped wedge finally gave up half a million dollars.

When activity moved west to Alaska three Australians, Jock, the Swagman, and the Dingo, bought a 12-month lease on Beach No. Two in Nome, nearly ran out of money unsuccessfully working it but agreed to continue after a speculative draw of cards, got down to their last day of funds when they found gravel and sand glittering with gold at the bottom of their shaft, and took out $413,000 in gold during their last thirty days.

Captain E. W. Johnson swapped a troublesome launch for a mining claim in Nome that so far had been unproductive, had so little luck with it that he turned the operation temporarily over to his father-in-law, J. L. Pidgeon, who immediately hit a pay streak. Within two years the mine yielded over $1½ million.

And so through the centuries luck has continued to play its part in the discovery of precious metals. Mines in India were found as the result of glimpsing the yellow metal in the mounds of dirt thrown up by nest-digging ants. As recently as 1933 in western Australia, a rich gold find resulted from testing a heap of dirt from a rabbit burrow. A woman lost her footing in Wales and laid bare a vein of rich ore. Gold mines in Spain were discovered when ploughmen turned up gleaming nuggets.

Back in this country at Cripple Creek, Colorado, so the story goes, a prospector built an enclosure for his campfire with rocks containing telluride minerals, only to discover their richness when the heat released the tellurium as gas, leaving behind drops of gold. Where Columbia in California's Mother Lode country produced millions of dollars in the lusty decade beginning in 1850, Dr. Thaddeus Hildreth, his brother George, and several other prospectors found gold while drying their blankets after a rainstorm, and another stampede was on.

California has been especially rich in finds. Where Elisha Holmes had homesteaded in Divine Gulch, his grandson, tilling the family garden years later, came across a gold nugget worth more than $1,000 which was only the start of that afternoon's riches. Angel's Camp, notorious in the state's mining history, was reborn as a stampede town when a prospector called Raspberry fired his rifle to free a wedged ramrod. The metal scraped a rock, revealing a clear yellow streak. And the Big Blue Mine, which headed the gold stampeders toward Quartzburg, was staked when Lovely Rogers heaved a rock at an erring mule and hit a vein of brightly flecked quartz instead.

Pack animals were responsible for the discovery of more than one mine. A wandering burro which sought shelter beneath a dark outcrop in Nevada is given the credit for the finding by Jim Butler of the Tonopah mine, the vein in the rock eventually giving up some $150 million in gold and silver. Then there's the white donkey of Noah Kellogg, wandering off during the night into a canyon in Idaho's Coeur d'Alenes, who was found the next morning lollling on one body of ore and gazing at another which gleamed like a mirror on the other side of the cut, thus reputedly beginning the history of the Bunker Hill mine, one of the world's richest producers of silver and lead.

Meanwhile, George Jackson started the whole "Pike's Peak or Bust" stampede, which uprooted hundreds of Easterners and sent them rumbling westward in covered wagons, by panning some dirt in one of the iron treaty cups with which the Government sought to pacify the Indians who saw more and more of their privacy giving way to gold seekers. One of these invaded sanctuaries was the Black Hills of South Dakota.

"Toward spring, in the latter part of March or in April," described Moses Manuel, "four of us found some rich float quartz. We looked for the lode, but the snow was deep and we could not find it. When the snow began to melt I wanted to go up and hunt it up again, but my three partners wouldn't look for it as they did not think it was worth anything. I kept looking every day for nearly a week, and finally the snow melted on the hill, and the water ran through the draw which crossed the lead, and I saw some quartz in the bottom with water running over it.

"I took a pick and tried to get some out and took it to camp and pounded it up and panned it and found it very rich. Next day Hank Harney consented to come and located what we called Homestake, the 9th of April, 1876. We started to dig a discovery shaft on the other side of this little draw, and the first chunk of quartz weighed about 200 pounds and was the richest ever taken out. We came over the next day

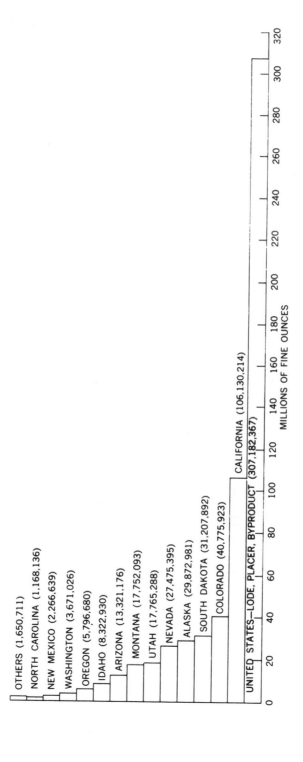

OTHERS (1,650,711)

NORTH CAROLINA (1,168,136)

NEW MEXICO (2,266,639)

WASHINGTON (3,671,026)

OREGON (5,796,680)

IDAHO (8,322,930)

ARIZONA (13,321,176)

MONTANA (17,752,093)

UTAH (17,765,288)

NEVADA (27,475,395)

ALASKA (29,872,981)

SOUTH DAKOTA (31,207,892)

COLORADO (40,775,923)

CALIFORNIA (106,130,214)

UNITED STATES—LODE, PLACER, BYPRODUCT (307,182,367)

MILLIONS OF FINE OUNCES

0   20   40   60   80   100   120   140   160   180   200   220   240   260   280   300   320

and ran an open cut and found we had a large deposit of a rich grade ore. After we built a road to Whitewood and bought an ox team and wagon, we built an arrista and hauled the gold over."

An arrista was a Spanish device used for the free milling of gold, being a circular pit whose bottom was tightly lined with rock over which heavy boulders were dragged, generally by a horse or mule, to grind the ore. The following winter they took out $5,000 by means of this. By autumn, though, the brothers and their partners had added a claim next to Homestake that began bringing in ore as rich as that of the original find, and a 10-stamp mill had been put up by Moses Manuel to replace the arrista.

Late in June 1877, George Hearst, father of the late William Randolph Hearst of newspaper fame, came into the Black Hills for a look at the Manuel operation and dickered for its purchase for $70,000. The brothers had already sold two other claims for an additional $80,000. It looked like they had made a fortune, but by 1920 the resulting Homestake Mining Company had uncovered nearly $60 million in gold, and by 1924 had produced roughly 90 percent of the more than $230 million of yellow metal brought out of the Black Hills since 1876. Homestake, still the richest working mine on the continent, is now yielding in the $1 billion range.

So it goes. Looking ahead at the start of this decade and seeing another ten years of inflation and controlled chaos, one economist found little merit in long-term municipal bonds, the previously established choice of numerous conservative investors. He suggested the difference between the Titanic and one of the better-known bond-floating cities is that the Titanic had a better orchestra.

"You have to choose between trusting in the natural stability of gold and the honesty and intelligence of members of the government," George Bernard Shaw once said. "And with due respect for these gentlemen, I advise you as long as the capitalistic system lasts to vote for gold."

Besides, as Agricola wrote centuries ago, "The occupation of the miner is objectionable to no one. For who, unless he is malevolent and envious, will hate the man who gains wealth as it were from heaven."

Chapter Two

BE A GOLD DIGGER

"BELL, BOOK AND candle shall not drive me back," wrote William Shakespeare, "when gold and silver becks me to come on."

American non-monetary consumption of gold has been three to four times greater than domestic production for several years, and the United States is unlikely to become self-sufficient in gold in the foreseeable future.

U. S. use of gold in industry and the arts has been running between six and seven million ounces annually during recent years, a typical breakdown being: jewelry and arts 60%, industry 29%, and dentistry 11%. All these non-monetary utilizations of the precious metal are rising steadily; in the arts and dentistry because of population growth and increasing affluence, and in industry, for fabrication of semiconductors, printed circuits, connectors, and other microcomponents for computer and space application. Non-monetary use of gold in the rest of the world is estimated at three to four times that of this country. The point is, gold has no entirely suitable substitute for any of its major functions.

The ceaseless need for it as well as for all other types of minerals gives weight to the surmise of Howard A. Meyerhoff, the executive director of the Scientific Manpower Commission, that despite the reawakened calls for conservation "the United States has become too concerned about how much of our mineral resources have been used and has paid too little attention to how much more we can find."

Gold is known to have been mined in substantial amounts for at least 6,000 years, likely first in Egypt where golden articles appeared as early as 4,000 B.C. It has always been in the thoughts of civilized man, going back to Homer's epic of Jason's odyssey in search of the golden apples of the sun and the golden fleece—the latter not being so far fetched as it might first seem, fleece being used by early sluicers to entrap the heavy metal.

And gold is heavy, having a density of 19.3 grams per cubic centimeter. This is twice that of lead and is exceeded only by some of the platinum metals and by rhenium, a rare metallic element that resembles manganese and is obtained either as a powder or as a heavy silver-white metal.

Gold, incidentally, is weighed in troy ounces, one troy ounce being 31.1 grams or 20 pennyweights. One metric ton of gold equals 32,150 ounces or 1.1 short tons. The expression "1 ppm" means one part per million and is the equivalent of one gram or 0.032 ounces per ton. The term "1 ppb" denotes one part per billion and equals 0.001 gram per ton.

When gold sold for $35 after devaluation during the 1930's, one gram was worth $1.12. At $100 an ounce, that same gram is worth $3.22, and more and more deposits which once had to be passed by as being uneconomical to mine have become rich.

Gold is at once soft, extremely malleable and most easily shaped, and at the same time highly resistant to corrosion and tarnish. Because of its workability, beauty, durability, and common occurrence as a native metal, gold was one of the first metals used by man. Over the centuries it has been a major medium of international monetary exchange, while its physical properties have brought it to be prized for jewelry and other adornments.

Gold has been traditionally equated with wealth, and the lore of lost gold mines and hidden pirate hoards cannot be matched by that about any other commodity. Even today gold is being sought more and more by the weekend prospector in the hope of striking it rich, as a few of his ancestors did here a century ago. Various estimates of the amount of gold mined since Columbus rediscovered the New World in 1492 converge at about 2½ billion ounces.

A reasonable guess about earlier production leads to an estimated total production throughout world history of about 3 billion ounces. Because if its indestructibility except in aqua regia, a mixture of nitric and hydrocholoric acids which also dissolves platinum, its appeal, and its intrinsic value, gold endures. Some has undoubtedly been lost in sunken ships, entombed with its owners, and hidden by people long dead, but a very large part of all that has ever been produced can be accounted for.

Official monetary reserves are about 1.3 billion ounces. The difference between this amount and the estimated total world production is some 1.7 billion ounces. This figure, less whatever gold still remains lost, gives an order of magnitude for the quantity of gold in jewelry, coin collections, museums, church adornments, electric equipment, capitol domes, teeth, and above all hoards in the forms of bars and coins. The amount is enormous, but some perspective may be gained from the fact that during 1966-67 alone, all newly mined gold, some 120 million ounces exclusive of the U.S.S.R., plus about 66 million ounces from non-Communist official reserves, passed into private holdings.

It is estimated that some 350 million ounces of gold are held in hoards alone. By way of contrast, this country's monetary reserves of gold at the end of 1971 totaled only 291.6 million ounces. U. S. known gold reserves of a few tens of millions of ounces are mainly in South Dakota's Homestake and Nevada's Carlin and Cortez gold deposits and in such copper accumulations as those in Bingham, Utah, which produce gold as a byproduct. The experts believe that gold deposits on this continent that remain as yet undiscovered are most likely to be those of widely dispersed gold, similar to Carlin and Cortez, which were overlooked in early prospecting.

A principal geologic problem related to U. S. gold deposits is the geologic and geochemical nature of the disseminated (Carlin-type) deposits. Inasmuch as these deposits likely represent the biggest relatively high grade resources of the United States, further research on them would seem to have a high potential payoff. Much is already known about the geologic settling and the geochemical makeup of these deposits, according to the U. S. Geological Survey, and they are the subject of continuing research. Nevertheless, no new discoveries have been reported since Cortez, Nevada, in 1966. Is some vital clue perhaps being overlooked?

The greatest gold-producing district in the world is the Witwatersrand in South Africa. Counterparts of the Precambrian gold-uranium placer deposits of the Rand seem to be very rare, and none even remotely comparable in productivity has ever been found. What critical combination of geologic factors was operative in the formation of these deposits? If this question could be answered satisfactorily, would it be possible to predict where and when other such combinations may have occurred in the past?

Extremely large amounts of gold must have been eroded from the Precambrian deposits of the Canadian Shield in Ontario and Quebec, yet very little gold has been found in the younger rocks overlying the Shield along its southern edge even though these were extensively sampled in the Heavy Metals Program tackled early in 1966 by the U. S. Geological Survey. Are there any more likely places where this gold may have been concentrated?

The high concentration of major gold deposits in rocks of the intermediate Precambrian age (2,700-1,600 million years) has already been noted. Many of these deposits are in rocks of, or related to, the so-called greenstone-granite association as in districts in Ontario and Quebec, Canada; Kalgoorlie, Australia; Kolar, India; and in Rhodesia. Do the auriferous greenstone-granite terrains have any geochemical peculiarities that would distinguish them from barren terrains with otherwise similar rock formations?

Broad alteration halos surround bonanza-type gold deposits. Much is being done to characterize these halos chemically and to determine the chemical and mineralogical changes that occur during the formation of a halo and its subsequent weathering. Will it be possible to distinguish a halo associated with an ore deposit from one in barren rock?

Gold deposits occur in mountain ranges at or near enough to the surface to be detected with existing exploration tools. But what of those deposits that doubtless exist in adjacent valleys beneath a thick cover of younger sediment? Can exploration tools be developed to detect them? Measurement of the mercury content of the air, which is higher over certain types of ore deposits, holds promise, for instance. Are there other elements that may be useful?

A group of related problems concerns the distribution of gold in rocks. Considerable information is available on the gold content of various rock types and minerals and of bedrock ores, but many gaps in knowledge remain. For example, there seem to be three points, or relatively narrow ranges of points, in the spectrum of gold concentrations: (1) crustal abundance of 0.003-0.004 ppm; (2) gold content of the lowest grade ore mined in modern times (Alaska Juneau mine) average grade of ore only about 0.04 oz. per ton and of porphyry copper deposits which yield gold as a byproduct (0.001-0.018 oz per ton); and (3) gold content of ore being mined at gold mines throughout the world (0.3-0/5 oz. per ton).

Is any appreciable percentage of the total gold in the accessible parts of the earth's crust present in concentrations intermediate between those of porphyry copper gold and currently mineable gold ore, or is there a real gap in the concentration range between those two grades of ore rather than only an apparent one created by mining economics? A corollary question concerns the distribution of gold near deposits of gold and other metals. Is gold confined largely to the deposits themselves or does it decrease gradually away from the deposits? That is, doesn't a gold-enriched halo or "assay wall" commonly bound a gold-bearing deposit?

Other gaps in knowledge include the mode of occurrence of gold in minerals, particularly those of mafic rocks (dark rocks rich in magnesium and iron) and the distribution of gold in porphyry copper deposits and their wall rocks.

Chapter Three

LODE AND PLACER GOLD

YOU CAN HAPPEN upon a gold strike while hunting, fishing, camping, or just plain hiking. The more you know about the subject, though, the better will be your chances. For example, your find can be one of two kinds, lode or placer. What is the difference? How did each chance to be?

The gold of primary deposits had been carried with other metals into the upper part of the earth's crust by rising warm or hot waters which, under pressure, follow fractures or cracks formed by the earth's movements. These cracks constitute the "plumbing system" along which solutions from greater depths can travel upward until they encounter cooler rocks. Generally, these latter areas are within a few thousand feet of the surface.

Where temperatures and pressures are less, minerals start to crystallize out of the solutions. The crystalline materials, including gold if this is present, accumulate along fracture surfaces and gradually fill voids along cracks to form veins. The solutions may continue upward, mingle with ground water, and emerge at the surface as hot springs.

Several theories are advanced by geologists to explain the origin of the mineralizing solutions. According to one hypothesis, solutions remaining or expelled from molten rock as it cooled and crystallized many thousands of feet below the earth's surface formed mineral deposits. These more volatile parts of the molten rock contain the heavy and precious metals, such as gold, and are among the last to crystallize.

Where cracks formed by the earth movements existed in and above the cooling molten rock, the more volatile mineralizing fractions escaped to the higher levels in the crust. The solution as expelled from the crystallizing liquid rock is chiefly water but carries with it silica and some metallic substances, including gold.

In a second hypothesis, the mineralizing solutions originated in sedimentary rock that contained entrapped water. Where sedimentary rocks are downfolded into the earth's crust and heated, the water is driven off. In its upward travel along fractures this dissolves metallic minerals from the rocks. In the cooler zones these are precipitated as vein materials.

According to a third theory, geologists surmise that when sedimentary rocks are deeply buried and subjected to heat and pressure, some of the water driven off was an integral part of the rock-forming minerals. These hot solutions also travel upward along fractures and deposit what are, in some cases, veins of gold.

Commonly, the principal constituents of a fracture filling or vein are quartz, or quartz and calcite, but the vein materials generally also contain some gold, copper, lead, iron, and other metal-bearing compounds. In many veins brasslike iron sulphide, pyrite, is abundant. Both this pyrite and iron-stained mica have sometimes been mistaken for gold and have been called "fool's gold."

PLACER GOLD

The gold in primary deposits is subject to weathering and erosion at the surface. During these processes, the rocks and the ore minerals in them are disintegrated into chunks, fragments, and finally into mineral grains. Products of this disintegration—boulders, gravel, sand, flakes, and finer particles—are washed into gullies, creeks, and rivers. Most mineral bearing rock fragments rapidly decompose chemically during weathering, and some of their constituents are dissolved and carried away by surface water. Gold, however, being extremely resistant, is carried downstream as metallic particles once it is freed from the enclosing rocks.

Both gold and coarse gravel can be moved only when water is running rapidly. On curves in streams where part of the current moves more slowly, or where the stream gradient is reduced, gold collects in sand and gravel bars. Gold, being about seven times heavier than gravel or sand, is quickly concentrated in the bed of a stream where it collects in low points and pockets. An irregular stream bed aids in trapping these gold particles. A few unusually heavy and resistant minerals commonly accumulate with gold. Magnetite is the most common, but other heavy minerals that may be present are platinum, cassiterite, monazite, ilmenite, columbite-tantalite, chromite, and some gem stones.

In gold-bearing country, gravel punchers, as they're called in parts of the Far North, look for gold where coarse sands and gravels have been concentrated and where they've settled with the gold. The natural processes of stream washing and wave action on beaches efficiently separate materials with different densities. These processes are similar in action to the prospector's pan and sluice box that sort and concentrate gold from lighter materials.

Placer deposits of gold have been formed in the same manner down through the globe's history. Throughout geologic time, the weathering and eroding processes have created some surface placer deposits which have been buried under rock debris. These fossil placer deposits are cemented into hard rocks by geologic action, yet the shape and the characteristics of the old river channels are still recognizable, like one just across the Peace River from my cabin where the Fraser River perhaps one time flowed.

In many areas the discovery of placer deposits has been the first clue to gold veins in the mountains in the headwaters of the stream. In some regions, however, the veins are too low grade for profitable mining, and deposits of economic value have been formed only where weathering and stream action have concentrated the vein gold into placer deposits. The richer gold placers have formed where a younger stream cut through an earlier placer deposit and concentrated the yellow metal for a second time.

WHO CAN FIND IT?

Increased leisure and more interest in outdoor living are leading more and more individuals and families to experiment with prospecting and even to go into small-scale gold production. Placer mining in particular has lured more than one person to try his luck and skill in the dream, sometimes fulfilled, of striking it rich. This is

particularly true now that you can sell gold on the free market for, at this writing, somewhat more than $180 an ounce.

Separating gold from embedded materials is basically simple and can be done effectively on nearly any scale, depending of course on the richness of the deposit and on the capital and time available for investment. The final product is consistently in demand, as it has been since the start of history.

However, although this is admittedly a way to turn a shoestring operation into a fortune, there are pitfalls when you pursue it strictly from a monetary viewpoint. The placer miner, for example, must know where placer deposits are located. So much country already has been explored that this is not an easy thing these days, although it is also true that many a deposit that would have been unprofitable when gold was pegged at from a fifth to a third of its present value will, if rediscovered today, sometimes prove a bonanza.

But he must have the technical knowledge and the stubbornness to extract the gold. Additionally, especially in this ecology-aware age, he must face problems of water pollution in addition to those of water supply and land ownership.

The costs of labor and equipment are relatively high now, although this may not seem significant to an individual mining a small deposit on his own. Too, secondhand equipment is frequently available, and you can still build your own gear from plans in this book, thus taking advantage of an opportunity that may sometimes make an otherwise unprofitable operation successful, at least as long as the outfit holds up.

Too, the novice or weekend prospector is often more interested in the recreational values offered by gold prospecting and mining than in its profitability. Although the casual miner may sell his gold, he often keeps it as a souvenir, for homemade jewelry, and as a certainly solid investment. Then there's all the unequaled pleasure, excitement, and satisfaction.

THE NEED FOR GOLD

Gold has been a precious material throughout history, eagerly sought and cherished. It was likely the first metal to be mined because it commonly occurs in its native form, because it is both beautiful and imperishable, and because exquisite objects can be formed from it even with primitive tools.

The amount of gold known to ancient civilization probably totaled not much more than the amount now produced each year from the world's largest gold mine, in the Witwatersrand district of South Africa, about a million-and-a-half ounces. Hoards of gold discovered by archeologists in Greece, Scythia, and Egypt, as well as the gold from Inca and Mayan treasuries in Mexico and Peru, represented years of patiently collecting small quantities from streams and veins, often by slave labor.

The intrinsic value of gold has always been recognized, even before gold was used in coinage, and it remains the only universally recognized standard of value. Most of the world's refined gold is absorbed by governments and central banks to provide stability for paper currency even though the world has gone off the so-called gold standard, but the amount of gold used in the arts and industry is increasing.

In addition to its use for jewelry, decorative finishes, and dentistry, its special properties have led to numerous applications in modern science and technology. Surface coatings of gold protect earth satellites from heat and corrison, and certain electrical components and circuits of spacecraft are made of gold when extreme precision and reliability are required.

WHERE

Gold was first produced in the United States from the southern Appalachian region, starting about 1792, but these deposits, though rich, were relatively small and quickly depleted. The finding of gold at Sutter's Mill in California sparked the gold rush of the Forty-Niners, and hundreds of mining camps sprang into being as new deposits were discovered. As a result, gold production increased swiftly.

The Mother Lode and Grass Valley mines in California and the Comstock Lode in Nevada were discovered during the 1860's, followed by the Cripple Creek deposits in Colorado in 1892. By 1905 the Tonopah and Goldfield deposits in Nevada and the Alaskan placer deposits had been uncovered, and gold production for the first time exceeded four million ounces a year, a level maintained until 1917.

During World War I and for some years thereafter, annual production declined to about two million ounces. When the price of gold was raised in 1934 to $35 an ounce, production increased rapidly and in 1937 again passed the four-million-ounce figure. Shortly after the start of World War II, gold mines were closed, and the government did not allow them to reopen until 1945. During 1965, about 1.68 million ounces of gold was produced, and by the end of that year the cumulative total of gold produced from deposits in the U.S. since 1792 had reached 307.2 million ounces.

The largest producing gold mine in the United States is the Home-Stake Mine at Lead, South Dakota, which yields about 575,000 ounces of gold each year. In this mine, which is more than a mile deep, hot mineral-bearing solutions formed primary deposits of gold and sulphide minerals.

The Carlin Mine near Carlin, Nevada, was opened in 1965 and is considered to be the largest gold discovery of the past half century. The discovery of this deposit, which contains an estimated $120 million in gold, was based on geologic investigations and interpretations published by the U. S. Geological Survey.

More than one-third of the gold produced in this country is a byproduct from mining other ores. Where base metals such as copper, lead, and zinc are deposited, either in veins or as scattered mineral grains, minor amounts of gold are usually lodged with them. Deposits of this kind are mined for the predominant metals, but during the processing the gold is also recovered.

Some deposits of base metals, such as disseminated or porphyry-copper deposits, are so large that even though they contain only a minor amount of gold per ton of copper ore, so much is mined that a substantial amount of gold is recovered. Gold taken from the copper ore mined at the vast open-pit mine at Bingham, Utah, for example, nearly equals the amount of gold produced from the biggest gold mine in the United States.

PLACER GOLD MINING HISTORY

Placer gold mining in this country spans a period of nearly two centuries. The earliest mining of record here took place in the eastern States and particularly in the southern Appalachian area during the latter 1700's and early 1800's, but the richer deposits were soon exhausted, and interest turned to the West. The earliest production of any note there was from the Old and New Placer Diggings near Golden in Santa Fe County, New Mexico, these deposits being worked as early as 1828.

A few other deposits were mined during the succeeding years until the first discovery of major importance, that of James Marshall on 24 January 1848 on the American River at Coloma, California. This find was a major factor in the rapid settlement of the West and set off the first of the great gold rushes in the U. S. Because of the lure and excitement of gold mining, prospectors spread throughout the West, and in subsequent years numerous additional rich placer deposits were uncovered.

Many placer deposits in California, the leading gold-producing state, have been mined on a large scale as recently as the mid-1950's. The streams that drain the rich Mother Lode—the Feather, Mokelumne, Calaveras, American, Consumnes, and Yuba Rivers—as well as the Trinity River in northern California, have a large amount of gold concentrate in their gravels. In addition, placers occur in the remnants of an older erosion cycle, the Tertiary gravels, in the same general areas.

The bulk of the gold mined in Alaska has come from placers which are widespread, occurring along nearly all the major rivers and their tributaries. The main placer-mining region has been the great Yukon River basin, which crosses central Alaska on its way from Canada and includes the extensive deposits around Fairbanks. Dredging in the Fairbanks district has produced more gold than in any other district in Alaska, and although it is predominantly a placer area, it also ranks high among the lode regions.

Any history of placer mining would be incomplete without a word on dredging which marked a major turn in operational efficiency. Dredging offered a way to handle tremendous quantities of material at a low unit cost and made it possible to mine where gold values were as little as a few cents per cubic yard. Likely the first successful bucketline dredge in the U. S. was operated in 1895 on Grasshopper Creek near Bannock in Beaverhead County, Montana.

Others rapidly followed until by 1910 the use of dredges had so increased that in California alone some 100 were in existence, of which 83 were reported to be in operation. The peak number, 149, was not reached until 1940. The Second World War then interrupted most operation. Costs rose beyond profitable levels after the conflict, and only a few of the deactivated dredges were returned to service.

The beach deposits in the Nome region, in the south-central part of the Seward Peninsula, rank second among productive placer deposits in the Forty-Ninth State. Other productive placers have been found in the drainage basin of the Copper River and of the Kuskokwim River.

In Alaska, as a matter of fact, gold occurrences were reported as early as 1848, and the yellow metal was found in the Yukon area about 1878. But it wasn't until the fabulously rich finds in 1897-98 in the Yukon's Klondike, just across the border in Canada, that placer miners really began to exploit the Alaskan deposits. In rapid succession, gravel punchers stampeded in 1898 to rich discoveries around Nome, then in 1902 to the country around thriving Fairbanks.

In Montana, the principal placer-mining districts are in the southwestern part of the State. Some of these more important localities are on the Missouri River in the Helena mining district where the famous Last Chance Gulch is located. Many regions are further south, on the headwaters and tributaries of the Missouri River, particularly in Madison County which ranks third in total gold production in Montana and which has produced more placer gold than any two other counties in the state.

The most productive placer deposit in Madison County, and in the entire state, has been that at Alder Gulch near Virginia City. Gold

has also been produced at many places on the headwaters of Clara Fork of the Columbia River, particularly in the vicinity of Butte, although in later years the placer output from this area has been overshadowed by the lode production.

A big proportion of the gold produced in Idaho has come from placer deposits, Idaho having been at one time one of the main placer-mining states. One of the chief dredging areas is in the Boise Basin, a few miles northeast of Boise, in the west-central part of the state. Other well-known placer localities are situated along the Salmon River in Lemhi and Idaho counties and on the Clearwater River and its tributaries, especially at Elk City, Pierce, and Orofino. Flour gold is found in the sands of the historic Snake River in southern Idaho.

Placers in Colorado have been highly productive in the Fairplay region in Park County and in the Breckenridge area in Summit County. In both districts large dredges were used during the peak activity of the 1930's. Colorado ranks second among the states in total gold production, with an aggregate of about 40,776,000 ounces through 1965.

In Oregon, the tributaries of the racing Rogue River and the neighboring streams in the Klamath Mountains have been the sources of placer gold. Among the major producing regions in this area are the Greenback district in Josephine County and the Applegate district in Jackson County. The most important mining areas of Oregon are in the northeastern portion of the state, where both placer and lode gold have been found. Placer gold occurs in numerous streams that drain the Wallows and Blue Mountains. One of the more productive placer regions in this area is in the vicinity of Sumpter, on the upper Powder River. The Burnt River and its tributaries have yielded gold. Farther to the West, placer mining has been carried on for many years in the John Day River valley.

Placer operations are not very important in the gold production of the other western mining states, although minor occurrences have been discovered in South Dakota—the Black Hills region, particularly in the Deadwood area and on French Creek, near Custer—as well as in Washington, on the Columbia and Snake Rivers.

In addition to the localities mentioned, placer gold has been found along many of the intermittent and ephemeral streams of arid regions in parts of Nevada, New Mexico, Arizona, and southern California. In many of these places a large reserve of low-grade ground still exists, but the lack of a permanent water supply necessitates the use of expensive dry and semi-dry concentration methods to recover the metal.

In the eastern states, limited amounts of gold have been washed from some of the streams that drain the eastern slopes of the southern Appalachian region, including parts of Virginia, Maryland, Alabama, Georgia, and North and South Carolina. Many saprolite deposits of this general region have also been mined by placer methods, and a small amount of gold has been obtained from placer deposits in tight little New England.

Some gold was produced in the East prior to the discovery of the California bonanzas. Other placer deposits in the East may be discovered. It is likely, however, that prospecting for them will require a substantial expenditure of money or at least time, as they probably will be low grade, difficult to recognize, and costly to explore and sample. Moreoever, at the present time ownership of all land in the East is such that claims may not be staked. In fact, prospecting can be legally carried out only with the permission of the owner of the property.

The following list includes essentially all the states and counties in which appreciable amounts of placer gold are known to occur.

Alabama: Chilton, Clay, Cleburne, Coosa, Randolph, Talladega.

Alaska: See map illustration for areas of occurrence.

Arizona: Conchise, Mohave, Pima, Yavapai, Yuma.

California: Amador, Butte, Calaveras, Del Norte, El Dorado, Fresno, Humboldt, Imperial, Kern, Los Angeles, Madera, Mariposa, Mono, Monterey, Nevada, Placer, Plumas, Sacramento, San Luis Obispo, Shasta, Sierra, Siskiyou, Trinity, Tuolumne, Yuba.

Colorado: Adams, Boulder, Chaffee, Clear Creek, Costilla, Eagle, Gilpin, Hinsdale, Jefferson, Lake, Mineral, Moffat, Montezuma, Park, Routt, San Juan, San Miguel, Summit.

Georgia: Barrow, Bibb, Carroll, Cherokee, Dawson, Douglas, Fannin, Forsyth, Fulton, Gilmer, Greene, Haralson, Hart, Henry, Lincoln, Lumpkin, Madison, Marion, McDuffie, Murray, Newton, Oglethorpe, Paulding, Rabun, Towns, Union, Walton, Warren, White, Wilkes.

Idaho: Ada, Adams, Bannock, Benewah, Boise, Bonneville, Camas, Cassia, Clearwater, Custer, Elmore, Idaho, Latah, Lemhi, Owyhee, Power, Shoshone, Twin Falls, Valley, Washington.

Montana: Beaverhead, Broadwater, Deer Lodge, Fergus, Granite, Jefferson, Judith Basin, Lewis and Clark, Lincoln, Madison, Meagher, Mineral, Missoula, Park, Powell, Silver Bow.

Nevada: Clark, Douglas, Elko, Esmeralda, Eureka, Humboldt, Lander, Mineral, Nye, Ormsby, Pershing, Washoe, White Pine.

New Mexico: Colfax, Grant, Lincoln, Otero, Rio Arriba, Sandoval, Sante Fe, Sierra, Taos.

North Carolina: Anson, Burke, Cabarrus, Caldwell, Catawba, Chatham, Cherokee, Clay, Cleveland, Davidson, Franklin, Gaston, Granville, Guilford, Halifax, Henderson, Iredell, Lincoln, Macon McDowell, Mecklenberg, Montgomery, Moore, Nash, Orange, Person, Polk, Randolph, Richmond, Rowan, Rutherford, Stanly, Union, Warren, Yadkin.

Oregon: Baker, Coos, Curry, Douglas, Grant, Jackson, Josephine, Union, Wheeler.

South Carolina: Cherokee, Chester, Chesterfield, Kershaw, Lancaster, Spartanburg, Union, York.

South Dakota: Custer, Lawrence, Pennington.

Utah: Beaver, Daggett, Garfield, Grand, Plute, Salt Lake, San Juan, Sevier, Uintah.

Virginia: Albemarle, Buckingham, Culpeper, Cumberland, Fluvanna, Goochland, Louisa, Spotsylvania, Stafford.

Washington: Chelan, Clallam Ferry, Kittitas, Lincoln, Okanogan, Whatcom.

LODE GOLD

Lode gold is metal in place within the solid rock where it has been deposited. Future discoveries of workable gold are likely to be made as a result of further investigations in areas already known to be productive.

Some of the more famous lodes include: in Alaska, around the magnificent once capital city of Juneau; in California, the Mother Lode, Grass Valley-Nevada City, and Allegheny districts; in Colorado, the Cripple Creek area and the districts of the San Juan region; in Nevada, the Goldfield and Comstock Lode country; and in the formerly Indian-fierce Black Hills of South Dakota, the Lead districts.

THE GOLD SEARCH CONTINUES

Geologists study all the factors that control the origin and emplacement of mineral deposits, including gold. Studies of igneous rocks in the field and in the laboratory lead to an understanding of how they crystallized to solid rock and how the mineral-bearing solutions and gases formed within them. Studies of rock structures such as folds, faults, joints, and fractures, and of the effects of pressure and heat on rocks, suggest why and where fractures of the crust took place and where veins may be found.

Knowledge of the chemical and physical characteristics of rocks yields information on the pattern of fractures and where to look for them. Studies of weathering processes and transport of materials by water enable geologists to predict the most likely places for placer deposits to form.

Research on prospecting methods had led to the development of mobile chemical and spectographic laboratories that are fitted with newly designed analytical instruments capable of detecting and rapidly measuring the amounts of gold and other valuable metals that may be present in rocks and ores. These labs can accompany the geologist into the field and, by providing on-the-spot analyses of selected samples, guide him in his search.

The occurrence of gold is not capricious. Its presence in various kinds of rocks and formation under differing environmental conditions follow natural laws. As geologists increase their knowledge of ore-forming processes they, and you can expect to improve the ability to find gold.

A chance for some degree of success by the individual prospector still remains, especially for those choosing favorable areas after a careful study of the mining record and the geology of the mining districts. It has been mainly to impart such information that the preceding brief review of various gold-mining regions has been presented.

Here, too, is a list of the geological agencies of the principal gold-producing States where additional information may be obtained:

Geological Survey of Alabama, University, Alabama 35486.

Alaska Division of Mines and Minerals, State Capitol Building, Juneau, Alaska 99801.

Arizona Bureau of Mines, University of Arizona, Tucson, Arizona 85721.

California Division of Mines and Geology, Department of Conservation, Ferry Building, San Francisco, California 94111.

Colorado Mining Industrial Development Board, 204 State Office Building, Denver, Colorado 80202.

Georgia Department of Mines, Mining and Geology, State Division of Conservation, 19 Hunter Street, S.W., Atlanta, Georgia 30303.

Idaho Bureau of Mines and Geology, University of Idaho, Moscow, Idaho 83844.

Montana Bureau of Mines and Geology, Montana College of Mineral Science and Technology, Butte, Montana 59701.

Nevada Bureau of Mines, Univesity of Nevada, Reno, Nevada 89507.

New Mexico State Bureau of Mines and Mineral Resources, New Mexico Institute of Mining and Technology, Socorro, New Mexico 87801.

North Carolina Division of Mineral Resources, Department of Conservation and Development, State Office Building, Raleigh, North Carolina 27600.

Oregon State Department of Geology and Mineral Industries, 1069 State Office Building, Portland, Oregon 97201.

South Carolina Division of Geology, State Development Board, P.O. Box 927, Columbia, South Carolina 29200.

South Dakota State Geological Survey, Science Center, University of South Dakota, Vermillion, South Dakota 57059.

Texas Bureau of Economic Geology, Univesity of Texas, Austin, Texas 78712.

Utah Geological and Mineralogical Survey, 103 Civil Engineering Building, University of Utah, Salt Lake City, Utah 84102.

Virginia Department of Conservation and Economic Development, Division of Mineral Resources, Natural Resources Building, Box 3667, Charlottesville, Virginia 22901.

Washington Division of Mines and Geology, Department of Conservation, 335 General Administration Building, Olympia, Washington 98501.

Geological Survey of Wyoming, University of Wyoming, Laramie, Wyoming 82070.

Chapter Four

WHERE TO LOOK
FOR PLACERS

PLACERS CAN BE found in virtually any area where lode gold occurs in hard rock deposits. The gold is released by weathering and by stream and glacier action, carried by gravel and water to some favorable point where, owing to its weight, it is deposited and concentrated in the process. Ordinarily the gold does not travel very far from the source, so knowledge of the location of the lode deposits can be useful. Gold also can be associated with copper and may form placers in the vicinity of copper deposits, although this happens less frequently.

The accompanying maps show where gold has been produced in the contiguous United States and in Alaska. And where, understandably, it was not always profitable to work deposits when gold was selling at $20 and even $35 an ounce, matters are different with the yellow metal now in the vicinity of $180 an ounce or more on the free market.

Geological events, including the raising and sinking of land such as the emergence of mountains and their rounding by wind and water, can cause prolonged and repeated cycles of erosion and concentration, and where these processes have happened placer deposits can be enriched.

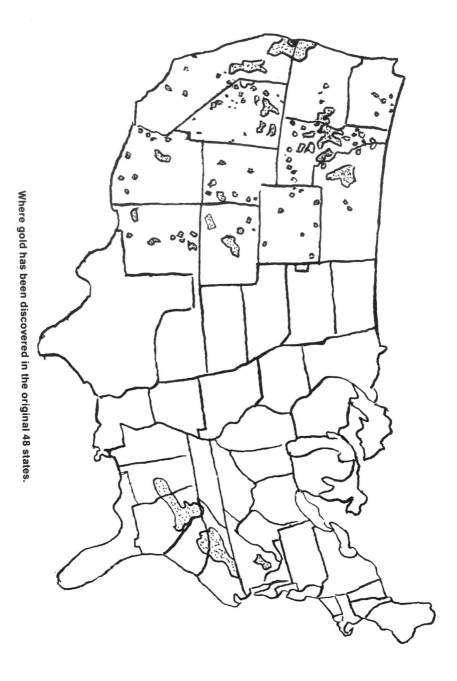

Where gold has been discovered in the original 48 states.

Ancient river channels, some of them on the tops of present mountains, and certain river bench deposits include examples of gold-bearing gravels that have been subjected to a number of such events, followed by at least their partial concealment by other deposits not excluding volcanic materials.

Residual placer deposits formed in the immediate vicinity of source rocks are ordinarily not the most productive, although exceptions occur where veins supplying the gold were exceptionally rich. Reworking of gold-bearing materials by stream action leads to the concentrations necessary for exploitation. In desert areas deposits may result from sudden flooding and washing out of intermittent streams.

As material gradually washes off the slopes and into streams, it becomes sort of stratified. Gold concentrates in so-called pay streaks with other heavy metals, among which the black, dense, magnetic, iron-filled magnetite is almost invariably present. The gold may not be entirely liberated from the original rock but may still have the white-to-grey vein quartz or other rock material attached to or enclosing it. As the gold moves downstream, it is gradually freed from the accompanying rock and flattened by the incessant pounding of gravel. Eventually it will become flakes and tiny particles, as the flattened pieces break up.

When it occurs with another element such as tellurium, some gold is not readily distinguishable by its normal qualities of high malleability and orange-yellow to light yellow metallic color. Upon weathering, such gold may be coated with a crust, as of iron oxide, and thus take on a rusty appearance. In placer operations this rusty gold, which resists amalgamation with mercury, may be overlooked or lost by careless handling.

As already suggested, the richest placers are not necessarily those occurring close to the source. Much depends upon how the placer materials were reworked by natural forces. Stream bed placers are the most important kind of deposit for the small-scale operator. Yet the gravel terraces and benches above the streams, as well as the ancient river channels that many times are concealed by later deposits, are potential sources of gold.

Other types of placers include those in the out-wash areas of streams where they enter other bodies of water, those at valleys, and those along the ocean front where beach deposits can be formed by the sorting action of waves and tidal currents. In desert areas, placers can be present along arroyos or gulches, or in built-up fans or cones below narrow canyons.

But although some gold may occur in the areas that form the upper parts of deltas, only fine gold can ordinarily be found here, there being little opportunity for its concentration because of the continual shifting of channels. Too, gold does not occur in the submerged portions of deltas. Pot holes and other low spots in the bedrock of a creek or river, furthermore, seldom show color inasmuch as they themselves are formed by erosion, and any gold brought into them by the current-carried gravel and sand is customarily ground fine and washed away.

The finding of gold in any placer is apt to be spotty. The coarse metal, ordinarily accompanied by some moderately rough or fine gold, can be scattered through the bottom 10 to 15 feet of gravels, particularly if they hold much clay or other fine material, but it is commonly concentrated at or close to bedrock. Too, streaks can be laid at any elevation in gravel on a false bottom of clay or other impervious material, not always in the deepest portion of the channel.

In narrow, V-shaped valleys, the pay dirt can well be scattered throughout the entire width of the bottom. In broad, flat valleys, on the other hand, the rich workings are more likely to be slimmer than the valley floor and to follow a line different from the present flowage. This is because the majority of gold-bearing gravels in wide valleys were originally built up in narrow valleys with comparatively high banks. As the slant decreased, the depression was widened by the wandering stream and buried beneath deepening clay, sand, gravel, and silt.

The course of a slowly flowing stream tends to stray, so that the substances in the valley floor are reworked numerous times. A pay streak may be moved by this reworking process, although if the gold is coarse or becomes hardened into place, it can stay in its original position while the stream meanders elsewhere. Gold-rich streams may split or end suddenly, inasmuch as gold concentrates mainly in such spots as the inside of curves where deposits are formed and eroded alternately and the bedrock acts as riffles.

The raising of the ground or some other geological circumstance can cause the stream to deepen its course, whereupon the former pay dirt can be worked into the new channel or stay in its former location to make a rich bench or old-channel placer. Barren gravel can be found, for that reason, at the bed of the present valley along rapids that are rimmed by one or several rock benches, while unusually rich diggings can sometimes be located where the water had eroded down under the original channel. The majority of rich placers are concentrations from tremendous volumes of rock found in areas that were first elevated, then cut by streams, and finally eroded for many thousands of feet to terrains of relatively low elevations.

Because gold is comparatively heavy, it tends to be found close to bedrock unless intercepted by layers of clay or compacted silts. It often works its way into cracks and crevices in the bedrock itself. Where the surface of the bedrock is highly irregular, the distribution of the gold will be uneven, although such a natural rifflelike surface favors accumulation.

Gold will amass at the head or foot of a bar, on bends where the current is slowed, and at the bottom of rapids where the stream gradient is reduced. Pockets behind boulders and other obstructions, even moss-covered sections of bank, can be places to look for deposits. Best results generally come from materials taken just above bedrock. The black sands that accumulate with gold are an excellent indicator of where to search.

Every year a certain amount of gold is washed down and redeposited during the spring runoffs, so it can be productive to rework some deposits periodically. This applies mainly to the near-surface materials such as those left on stream bars and in sharp depressions in channels. The upstream ends of the bars are especially productive. Where high water has washed across a surface by the shortest route, as along the inside of a bend, enrichment often results. A rifflelike surface here will enhance the possibility of gold concentration.

In prospecting areas with a history of mining, try to find spots where mechanized mining had to stop because of an inability to follow erratic portions of rich pay streaks without great dilution from nonpaying materials. Smaller scale, selective mining may still be practical here if a prospector is diligent.

ALASKA

The majority of Alaska's gold production has come from placers, mainly those in the Yukon River Basin, although as shown by the map deposits are known on nearly all major rivers and their tributaries. Beach deposits in the Nome area have been notably productive, as have the river and terrace or bench placers in the drainage of the Kuskokwin and Copper Rivers. Climatic conditions play a great part in Alaskan mining, and the season for hydraulic operations of any kind is relatively short.

CALIFORNIA

California has led all other states in placer mining and as would be expected has many gold-producing areas of interest, including

Gold-mining districts of Alaska.

Cook Inlet-Sustina region:
1, Kenai Peninsula; 2, Valdez Creek; 3, Willow Creek; 4, Yentna-Cache Creek.

Copper River region:
5, Chistochina; 6, Nizina.

Kuskokwim region:
7, Georgetown; 8, Goodnews Bay; 9, McKinley; 10, Tuluksak-Aniak.

Northwestern Alaska region:
11, Shungnak.

Seward Peninsula region:
12, Council; 13, Fairhaven; 14, Kougarok; 15, Koyuk; 16, Nome; 17, Port Clarence; 18, Solomon-Bluff.

Southeastern Alaska region:
19, Chichagof; 20, Juneau; 21, Ketchikan-Hyder; 22, Porcupine; 23, Yakataga.

Southwestern Alaska region:
24, Unga.

Yukon region:
25, Bonnifield; 26, Chandalar; 27, Chisana; 28, Circle; 29, Eagle; 30, Fairbanks; 31, Fortymile; 32, Iditarod; 33, Innoko; 34, Hot Springs; 35, Kantishna; 36, Koyukuk; 37, Marshall; 38, Nabesna; 39, Rampart; 40, Ruby; 41, Richardson; 42, Tolovana.

Prince William Sound region:
43, Port Valdez.

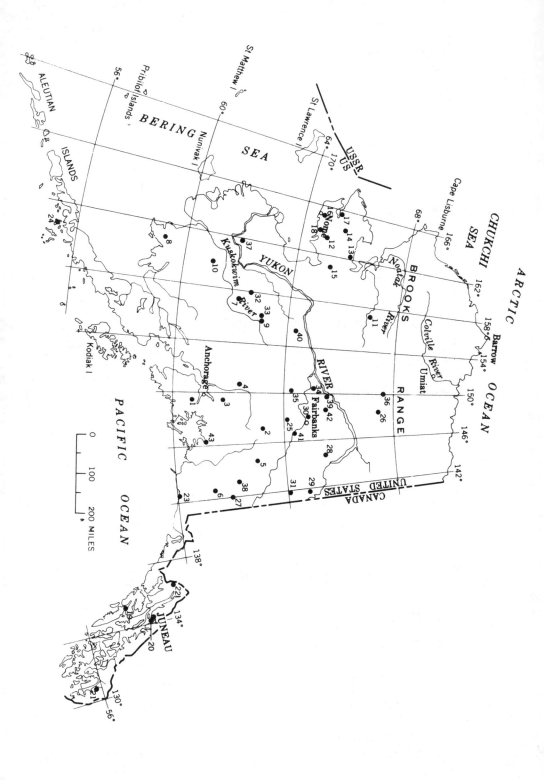

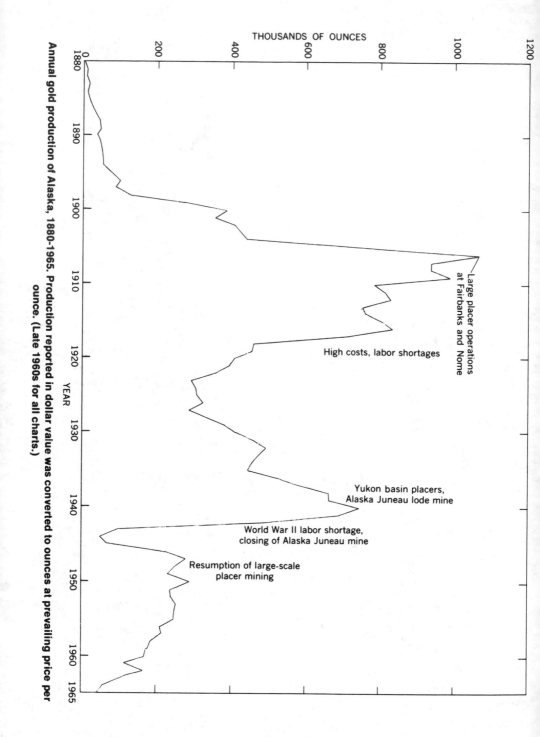

THOUSANDS OF OUNCES

Large placer operations
at Fairbanks and Nome

High costs, labor shortages

Yukon basin placers,
Alaska Juneau lode mine

World War II labor shortage,
closing of Alaska Juneau mine

Resumption of large-scale
placer mining

YEAR

Annual gold production of Alaska, 1880-1965. Production reported in dollar value was converted to ounces at prevailing price per ounce. (Late 1960s for all charts.)

especially gravels enriched by the Mother Lode system of gold deposits, a strip of mineralized rock one to four miles wide that extends 120 miles along the lower western flank of the Sierra Nevada, traversing five counties—El Dorado, Amador, Calaveras, Tuolumne, and Mariposa.

Ancient channels and gravels of the Sierra Nevada Range have been particularly productive sources of the yellow metal, and maps have been published by the California Division of Mines and Geology, 1416 Ninth Street, Sacramento 95814 showing the approximate routes of these features. Two maps of the U.S. Forest Service, Washington, D.C. 20250 that the prospector would find of especial value in considering the Sierra deposits are (1) the Downieville, Camptonville, and Nevada City districts, Tahoe National Forest; and (2) the Foresthill and Big Bend districts, also in the Tahoe National Forest. Maps covering the Trinity and Klamath National Forests of northern California might also be of interest.

COLORADO

A few important Colorado placers of the residual type are found on slopes and hillsides in the immediate vicinity of gold veins. However, placers in Colorado are confined generally to narrow canyons below lode gold mining areas within the Rocky Mountains in a belt which slants northeast across the western part of the state.

Almost every gold district has had some placer production. Many of the streams emerging from the Front Range, the headwaters of the South Platte River, and the Arkansas River and its tributaries as far upstream as California Gulch contain placer gold. Historically, placers were mined first and led to the development of Colorado's rich lodes.

IDAHO

The Boise basin, northwest of that city, is noted in Idaho for the dredging of placers. Other well-known placer areas lie along the Salmon River in Lemhi and Idaho counties and on the Clearwater River and its territories, especially in the vicinity of Elk City, Pierce, and Orodine. Placer gold is also found along the Snake River, but this is commonly fine-grained or flour gold that is difficult to recover.

Gold-mining districts of California.

Amador County:
1, Mother Lode; 2, Fiddletown; 3, Volcano; 4, Cosumnes River placers.

Butte County:
5, Magalia; 6, Oroville; 7, Yankee Hill.

Calaveras County:
8, Mother Lode, East Belt, and West Belt; 9, Placers in Tertiary gravels; 10, Jenny Lind; 11, Camanche; 12, Campo Seco.

Del Norte County:
13, Smith River placers.

El Dorado County:
14, Mother Lode, East Belt, and West Belt; 15, Georgia Slide; 16, Placers in Tertiary gravels.

Fresno County:
17, Friant.

Humboldt County:
18, Klamath River placers.

Imperial County:
19, Cargo Muchacho.

Inyo County:
20, Ballarat; 21, Chloride Cliff; 22, Resting Springs; 23, Sherman; 24, Union; 25, Wild Rose; 26, Willshire-Bishop Creek.

Kern County:
27, Amalie; 28, Cove; 29, Green Mountain; 30, Keyes; 31, Rand; 32, Rosamond-Mojave; 33, Joe Walker mine; 34, St. John mine; 35, Pine Tree mine.

Lassen County:
36, Diamond Mountain; 37, Hayden Hill.

Los Angeles County:
38, Antelope Valley; 39, Acton; 40, San Gabriel.

Mariposa County:
41, Mother Lode, East Belt; 42, Mormon Bar; 43, Hornitos; 44, Merced River placers; 45, Placers in Tertiary gravels.

Merced County:
46, Snelling.

Modoc County:
47, High Grade.

Mono County:
48, Bodie; 49, Masonic.

Napa County:
50, Calistoga.

Nevada County:
51, Grass Valley-Nevada City; 52, Meadow Lake; 53, Tertiary placer districts.

Placer County:
54, Dutch Flat-Gold Run; 55, Foresthill; 56, Iowa Hill; 57, Michigan Bluff; 58, Ophir; 59, Rising Sun mine.

Plumas County:
60, Crescent Mills; 61, Johnsville; 62, La Porte.

Riverside County:
63, Pinacate; 64, Pinon-Dale.

Sacramento County:
65, Folsom; 66, Sloughhouse.

San Bernardino County:
67, Dale; 68, Holcomb; 69, Stedman.

San Diego County:
70, Julian.

San Joachin County:
71, Clements; 72, Bellota.

Shasta County:
73, Deadwood-French Gulch; 74, Igo; 75, Harrison Gulch; 76, West Shasta; 77, Whiskeytown.

Sierra County:
78, Alleghany and Downieville; 79, Sierra Buttes.

Siskiyou County:
80, Humbug; 81, Klamath River; 82, Salmon River; 83, Scott River; 84, Cottonwood-Fort Jones-Yreka.

Stanislaus County:
85, Oakdale-Knights Ferry; 86, Waterford.

Trinity County:
87, Trinity River; 88, Carrville.

Tulare County:
89, White River.

Tuolumne County:
90, Mother Lode; 91, East Belt; 92, Pocket Belt; 93, Columbia Basin-Jamestown-Sonora; 94, Groveland-Moccasin-Jacksonville.

Yuba County:
95, Browns Valley-Smartville; 96, Brownsville-Challenge-Dobbins; 97, Hammonton.

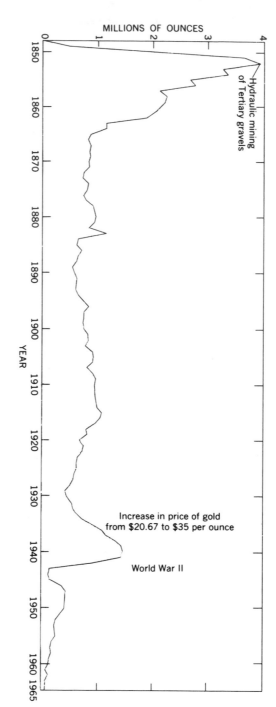

Annual gold production of California, 1848-1965.

MONTANA

The Helena mining district and the many placers along the great Missouri River in the vicinity of Helena and upstream are among the more important areas. The headwaters and tributaries of this same stream in Madison County, particularly near Virginia City and Bannack, are noted for early placer production. Placer gold has also been uncovered on the headwaters of the Clark Fork of the Columbia River at a number of points.

NEVADA

Some 115 placer districts in Nevada are estimated to have produced a minimum of 1,700,000 ounces of placer gold from 1948 to 1968, the largest such production in the Southwest. Yet, although potential sources in the form of lode gold are widely distributed throughout the state, Nevada has not been as large a producer of placer riches as it would have been if water were not so relatively scarce. In the past dry washers, as well as other methods that are very conservative of water, have been used extensively.

Producing areas have been largely found in the western half of the state and include Spring Valley and American Canyon in the Humboldt Range, Pershing County, and Manhattan and Round Mountain areas of Nye County. Placers have also been worked below Virginia City and near Charleston in northern Elko County. Signs of limited placer diggings may be seen in numerous parts of the state.

The production of precious metals in Nevada has been approximately one billion dollars, of which about 40 percent has been in gold and the rest silver. In comparison with the gold production from lode mines, the placer product of $30,000,000 appears trifling, amounting to about 7 percent.

NEW MEXICO

Although New Mexico has been thoroughly prospected for gold deposits since 1828, there is indication that not all the placer deposits have been completely explored or exploited. Apparently unmined placer deposits have been found in the Jicarilla, Old Placers, Orogande, Hopewell, Pittsburg, and Millsboro districts, and extensive testing of these unmined gravels might reveal large tonnages of suitable grade to warrant future mining.

Gold-mining districts of Colorado.

Adams County:
  1, Clear Creek placers.
Boulder County:
  2, Jamestown; 3, Gold Hill-Sugarloaf; 4, Ward; 5, Magnolia; 6, Grand Island-Caribou.
Chaffee County:
  7, Chalk Creek; 8, Monarch.
Clear Creek County:
  9, Alice; 10, Empire; 11, Idaho Springs; 12, Freeland-Lamartine; 13, Georgetown-Silver Plume; 14, Argentine.
Custer County:
  15, Rosita Hills.
Dolores County:
  16, Rico.
Eagle County:
  17, Gilman.

Gilpin County:
  18, Northern Gilpin; 19, Central City.
Gunnison County:
  20, Gold Brick-Quartz Creek; 21, Tincup.
Hinsdale County:
  22, Lake City.
Jefferson County:
  23, Clear Creek placers.
Lake County:
  24, Leadville; 25, Arkansas River valley placers.
La Plata County:
  26, La Plata.
Mineral County:
  27, Creede.
Ouray County:
  28, Sneffels-Red Mountain; 29, Uncompahgre.

Park County:
  30, Alma; 31, Fairplay; 32, Tarryall.
Pitkin County:
  33, Independence Pass.
Rio Grande County:
  34, Summitville.
Routt County:
  35, Hahns Peak.
Saguache County:
  36, Bonanza.
San Juan County:
  37, Animas; 38, Eureka.
San Miguel County:
  39, Ophir; 40, Telluride; 41, Mount Wilson.
Summit County:
  42, Breckenridge; 43, Tenmile.
Teller County:
  44, Cripple Creek.

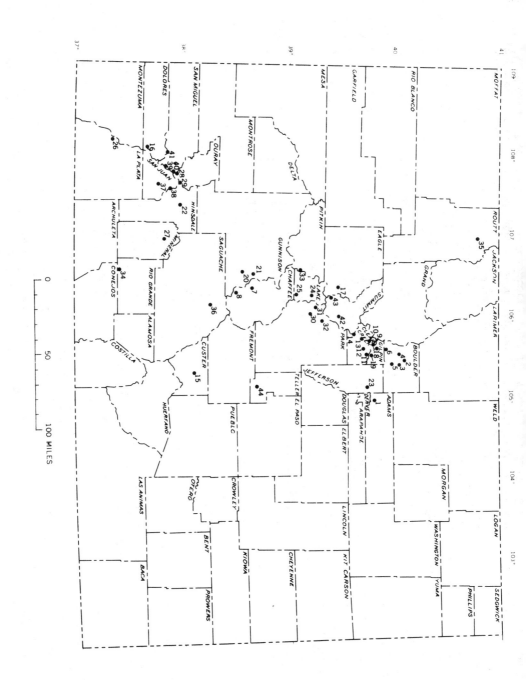

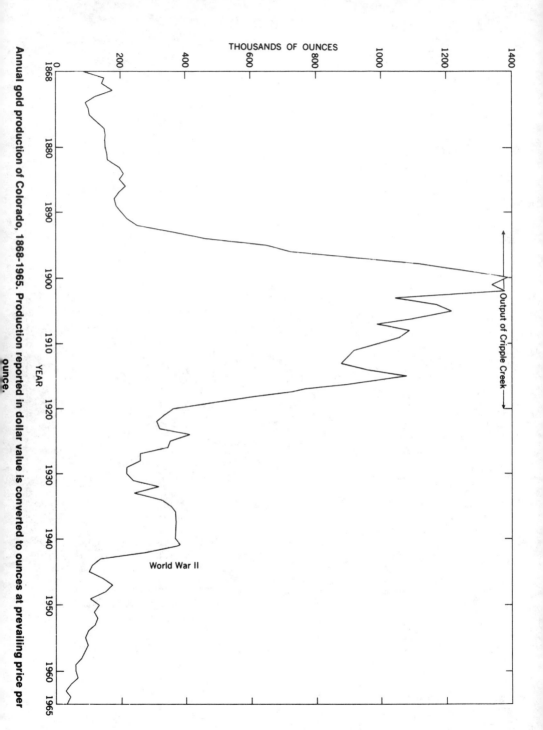

Annual gold production of Colorado, 1868-1965. Production reported in dollar value is converted to ounces at prevailing price per ounce.

OREGON

Oregon's placers are located mainly in the southwestern part of the state, on tributaries of the Rogue River and on streams in the Klamath Mountains. Major gold-producing areas are the Applegate district in Jackson County and the Greenback region in Josephine County. Placer gold also occurs in many of the streams that drain the Blue and Wallows Mountains in northeast Oregon. The Sumpter areas and the upper Powser River have had important production. Other country includes the John Day River Valley and the Burnt River and its tributaries.

UTAH

Although at least 85,000 ounces of gold have been produced from 18 major placer deposits in Utah, the "mother lode" sources of many of the concentrations remain unknown, according to a recent U.S. Geological Survey report.

The origin of the placer gold found along the Colorado River and its major tributaries is still not known. Incidentally, many of the gold-bearing sand bars along the Colorado and San Juan Rivers have been drowned by the rising waters of Lake Powell, formed by the Glen Canyon Dam in northern Arizona.

WASHINGTON

Washington is noted for placers, although gold has been found along a number of its streams, including some that ripple down the western slope of the Cascade Mountains. Generally, the few productive placers have been confined to the north-central portion of the state.

OTHER STATES

Among the other western states, placer mining has been limited to only a few localized areas. In South Dakota, the Black Hills, especially the Deadwood area, and French Creek near Custer have been productive sources. New Mexico and Arizona placers are in some instances related to copper deposits that carry gold.

In the eastern states, some of the streams draining the eastern slopes of the southern Appalachian Range have yielded gold. Saprolite deposits, rock decomposed at its original site, have been a source of placer

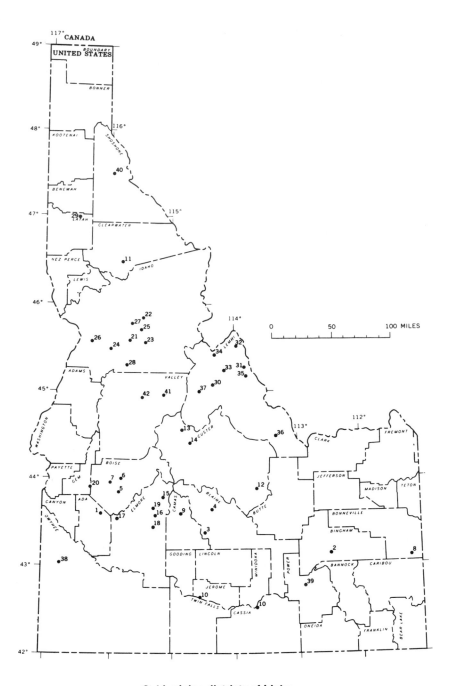

Gold-mining districts of Idaho.

Ada County:
1, Black Hornet.

Bingham County:
2, Snake River placers.

Blaine County:
3, Camas; 4, Warm Springs.

Boise County:
5, Boise Basin; 6, Pioneerville; 7, Quartzburg.

Bonneville County:
8, Mount Pisgah.

Camas County:
9, Big and Little Smoky-Rosetta.

Cassia, Jerome, and Minidoka Counties:
10, Snake River placers.

Clearwater County:
11, Pierce.

Custer County:
12, Alder Creek; 13, Loon Creek; 14, Yankee Fork.

Elmore County:
15, Atlanta; 16, Featherville; 17, Neal; 18, Pine Grove; 19, Rocky Bar.

Gem County:
20, Westview.

Idaho County:
21, Buffalo Hump; 22, Elk City; 23, Dixie; 24, French Creek-Florence; 25, Orogrande; 26, Simpson-Camp Howard-Riggins; 27, Tenmile; 28, Warren-Marshall.

Latah County:
29, Hoodoo.

Lemhi County:
30, Blackbird; 31, Carmen Creek-Eldorado-Pratt Creek-Sandy Creek; 32, Gibbonsville; 33, Mackinaw; 34, Mineral Hill and Indian Creek; 35, Kirtley Creek; 36, Texas; 37, Yellow Jacket.

Owyhee County:
38, Silver City.

Power County:
39, Snake River placers.

Shoshone County:
40, Coeur d'Alene region.

Valley County:
41, Thunder Mountain; 42, Yellow Pine.

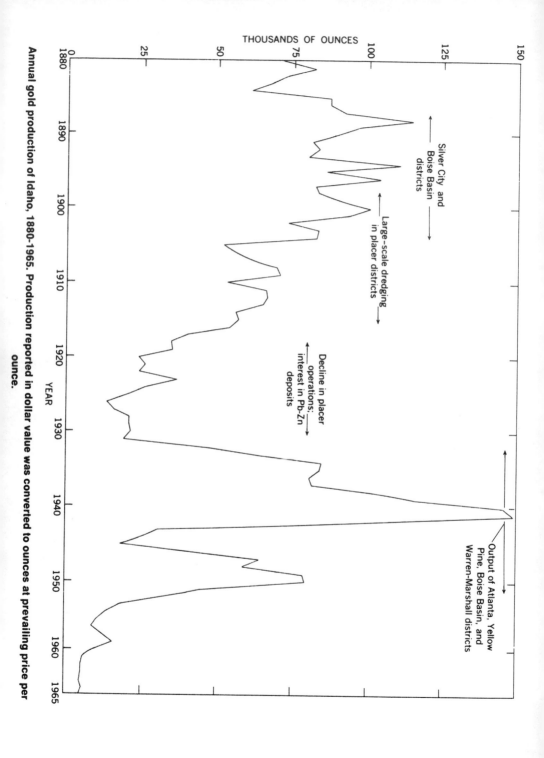

Annual gold production of Idaho, 1880-1965. Production reported in dollar value was converted to ounces at prevailing price per ounce.

THOUSANDS OF OUNCES

YEAR

Silver City and
Boise Basin
districts

Large-scale dredging
in placer districts

Decline in placer
operations;
interest in Pb-Zn
deposits

Output of Atlanta, Yellow
Pine, Boise Basin, and
Warren-Marshall districts

diggings in Georgia and the Carolinas. Generally, the eastern placers are sparsely distributed and the gold in them low grade. Thus, few serious efforts have been made at mining them since the early 1800's. Nevertheless, many locations offer possibilities for small operations at today's high prices if only primarily as sideline projects.

CANADA

The initial important placer deposit in Canada was in the country drained by the Chaudiere River southeast of Quebec, the capital city of that Province and a St. Lawrence River port. The initial find was made in 1823, but large-scale digging did not start until 1875 when difficulties were encountered because of the heavy overburden, the preponderance of huge boulders, and the slow running of the stream which made sluicing difficult. These hardships, in fact, limited exploitation, and there is still the possibility, especially with the present price of gold, that profitable occurrences of gold and other placer minerals exist here.

Gold has been found in many streams throughout New Brunswick, but here, too, because few people have searched specifically for the metal, possibilities are believed to be promising. It was away back in 1900 that a record yield of 33,955 ounces of gold was mined in Nova Scotia where rising costs of labor and materials finally brought an end to activities. In common with most Canadian gold occurrences, those in Newfoundland have suffered continental glaciation, and secondary enrichment is therefore of negligible importance and known gold placers are rare, although large parts of the island have not as yet been closely prospected.

The first significant gold discovery in British Columbia was in 1857 on the Thompson River, a tributary of the Fraser River where find after find was made after the news reached the miners in California. By 1860, the rush had reached the Cariboo district where placers eventually gave up over $50 million in the yellow metal although there is now little activity here. Gravel punchers pressed north from here and uncovered important placers in the Omineca, Cassiar, and Atlin regions of the Province where, too, little placer mining is still carried on.

Then the discovery of gold on Bonanza Creek, a tributary of the Klondike River just east of Alaska, set off in 1896 the biggest gold rush of them all, reaching a peak production of $22 million in 1900. Beyond a few other placer fields that were discovered afterwards in the Yukon Territory, the Peace and the North Saskatchewan Rivers

Gold-mining districts of Montana.

Beaverhead County:
  1, Bannack; 2, Argenta; 3, Bryant.

Broadwater County:
  4, Confederate Gulch; 5, White Creek; 6, Winston; 7, Park; 8, Radersburg.

Cascade County:
  9, Montana.

Deerl Lodge County:
  10, French Creek; 11, Georgetown.

Fergus County:
  12, Warm Springs; 13, North Moccasin.

Granite County:
  14, First Chance; 15, Henderson Placers; 16, Boulder Creek; 17, Flint Creek.

Jefferson County:
  18, Clancy; 19, Wickes; 20, Basin and Boulder; 21, Elkhorn; 22, Tizer; 23, Whitehall.

Lewis and Clark County:
  24, Rimini-Tenmile; 25, Helena-Last Chance; 26, Missouri River-York; 27, Sevenmile-Scratchgravel; 28, Marysville-Silver Creek; 29, Stemple-Virginia Creek; 30, McClellan; 31, Lincoln.

Lincoln County:
  32, Libby; 33, Sylvanite.

Madison County:
  34, Virginia City-Alder Gulch; 35, Norris; 36, Pony; 37, Renova; 38, Silver Star-Rochester; 39, Tidal Wave; 40, Sheridan.

Mineral County:
  41, Cedar Creek-Trout Creek.

Missoula County:
  42, Ninemile Creek; 43, Elk Creek-Coloma.

Park County:
  44, Emigrant Creek; 45, Jardine; 46, Cooke City.

Phillips County:
  47, Little Rocky Mountains.

Powell County:
  48, Finn; 49, Ophir; 50, Pioneer; 51, Zosell.

Ravalli County:
  52, Hughes Creek.

Silver Bow County:
  53, Butte; 54, Highland.

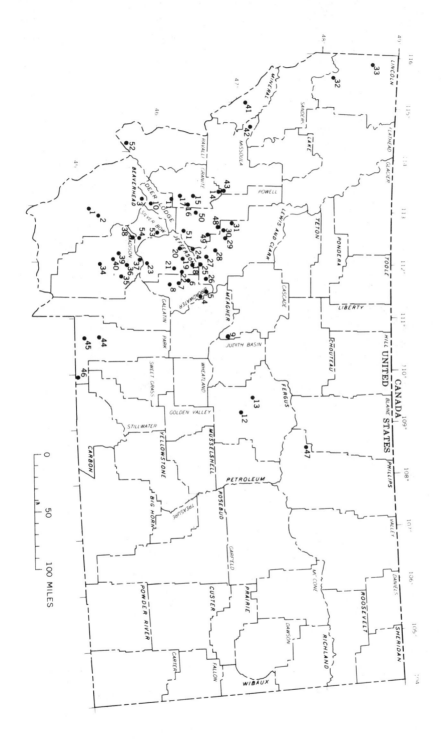

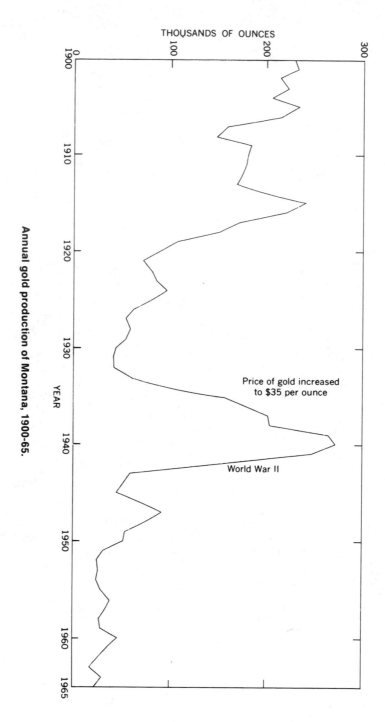

Annual gold production of Montana, 1900-65.

in British Columbia and Alberta have been the only other drainages in western Canada where placer mining has been successful to any extent.

The most likely regions in Canada to prospect successfully for placer gold, therefore, lie in those parts of the Yukon and northern British Columbia that have not been searched exhaustively, especially in those areas not swept by glaciers and where mineral-carrying metamorphic or igneous rocks occur to some extent.

Where the glaciers have ground past, slim, V-shaped valleys, particularly those rimmed by rock benches, should be given primary attention and those valleys rounded and eroded by severe glacial action bypassed.

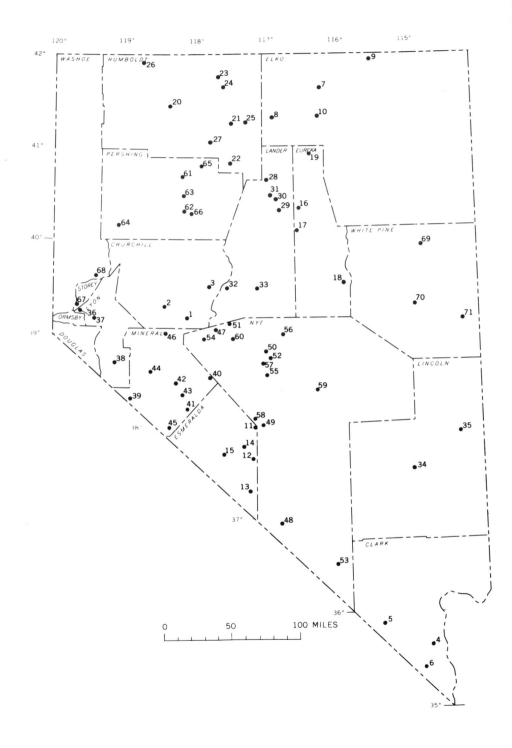

Gold-mining districts of Nevada.

Churchill County:
   1, Fairview; 2, Sand Springs; 3, Wonder.

Clark County:
   4, Eldorado; 5, Goodsprings; 6, Searchlight.

Elko County:
   7, Edgemont; 8, Gold Circle; 9, Jarbridge; 10, Tuscarora.

Esmeralda County:
   11, Divide; 12, Goldfield; 13, Hornsilver; 14, Lone Mountain; 15, Silver Peak.

Eureka County:
   16, Buckhorn; 17, Cortez; 18, Eureka; 19, Lynn.

Humboldt County:
   20, Awakening; 21, Dutch Flat; 22, Gold Run; 23, National; 24, Paradise Valley; 25, Potosi; 26, Warm Springs; 27, Winnemucca.

Lander County:
   28, Battle Mountain; 29, Bullion; 30, Hilltop; 31, Lewis; 32, New Pass; 33, Reese River.

Lincoln County:
   34, Delamar; 35, Pioche.

Lyon County:
   36, Silver City; 37, Como; 38, Wilson.

Mineral County:
   39, Aurora; 40, Bell; 41, Candelaria; 42, Garfield; 43, Gold Range; 44, Hawthorne; 45, Mount Montgomery and Oneota; 46, Rawhide.

Nye County:
   47, Bruner; 48, Bullfrog; 49, Ellendale; 50, Gold Hill; 51, Jackson; 52, Jefferson Canyon; 53, Johnnie; 54, Lodi; 55, Manhattan; 56, Northumberland; 57, Round Mountain; 58, Tonopah; 59, Tybo; 60, Union.

Pershing County:
   61, Humboldt; 62, Rochester; 63, Rye Patch; 64, Seven troughs; 65, Sierra; 66, Spring Valley.

Storey County:
   67, Comstock Lode.

Washoe County:
   68, Olinghouse.

White Pine County:
   69, Cherry Creek; 70, Ely; 71, Osceola.

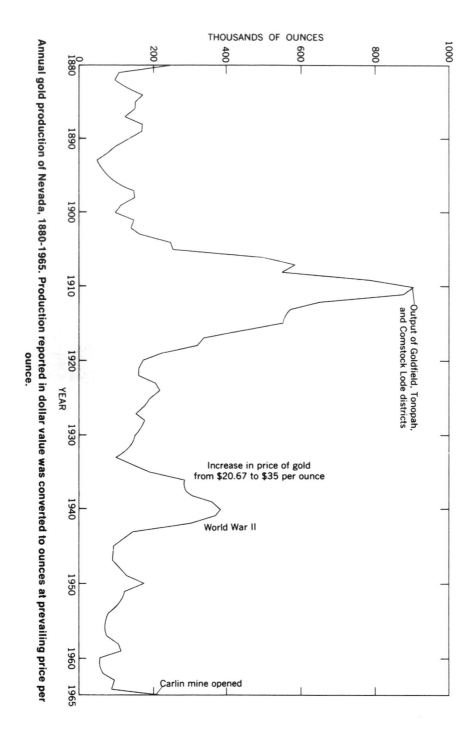

THOUSANDS OF OUNCES

Output of Goldfield, Tonopah, and Comstock Lode districts

Increase in price of gold from $20.67 to $35 per ounce

World War II

Carlin mine opened

YEAR

Annual gold production of Nevada, 1880-1965. Production reported in dollar value was converted to ounces at prevailing price per ounce.

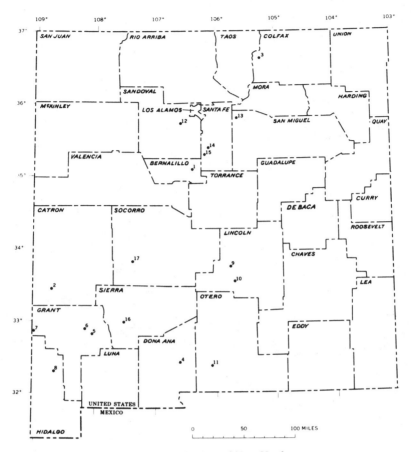

Gold-mining districts of New Mexico.

Bernalillo County:
1, Tijeras Canyon.
Catron County:
2, Mogollon.
Colfax County:
3, Elizabethtown-Baldy.
Dona Ana County:
4, Organ.
Grant County:
5, Central; 6, Pinos Altos; 7, Steeple Rock.
Hidalgo County:
8, Lordsburg.

Lincoln County:
9, White Oaks; 10, Nogal.
Otero County:
1, Jarilla.
Sandoval County:
12, Cochiti.
San Miguel County:
13, Willow Creek.
Santa Fe County:
14, Old Placer; 15, New Placer.
Sierra County:
16, Hillsboro.
Socorro County:
17, Rosedale.

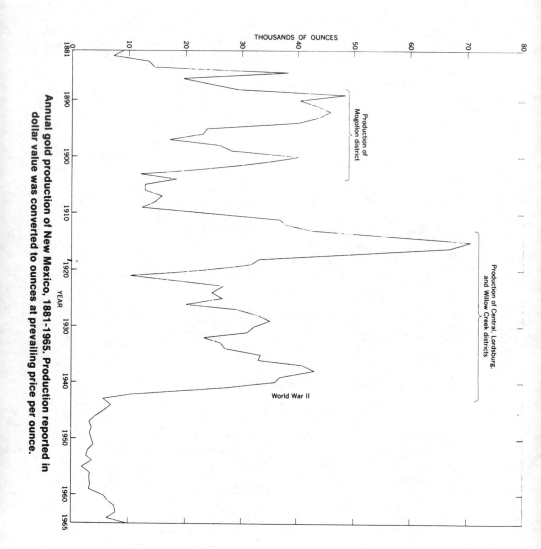

Annual gold production of New Mexico, 1881-1965. Production reported in dollar value was converted to ounces at prevailing price per ounce.

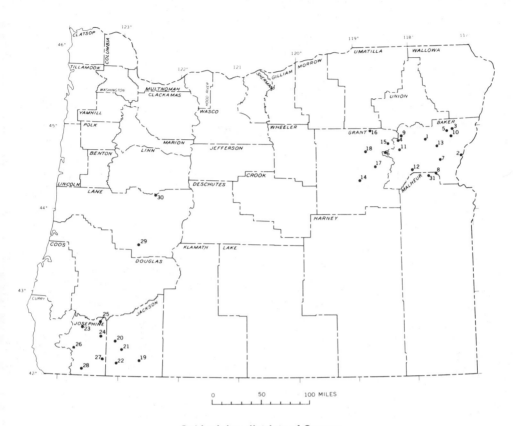

Gold-mining districts of Oregon.

Baker County:
1, Baker; 2, Connor Creek; 3, Cornucopia; 4, Cracker Creek; 5, Eagle Creek; 6, Greenhorn; 7, Lower Burnt River valley; 8, Mormon Basin; 9, Rock Creek; 10, Sparta; 11, Sumpter; 12, Upper Burnt River; 13, Virtue.

Grant County:
14, Canyon Creek; 15, Granite; 16, North Fork; 17, Quartzburg; 18, Susanville.

Jackson County:
19, Ashland; 20, Gold Hill; 21, Jacksonville; 22, Upper Applegate.

Josephine County:
23, Galice; 24, Grants Pass; 25, Greenback; 26, Illinois River; 27, Lower Applegate; 28, Waldo.

Lane County:
29, Bohemia; 30, Blue River.

Malheur County:
31, Malheur.

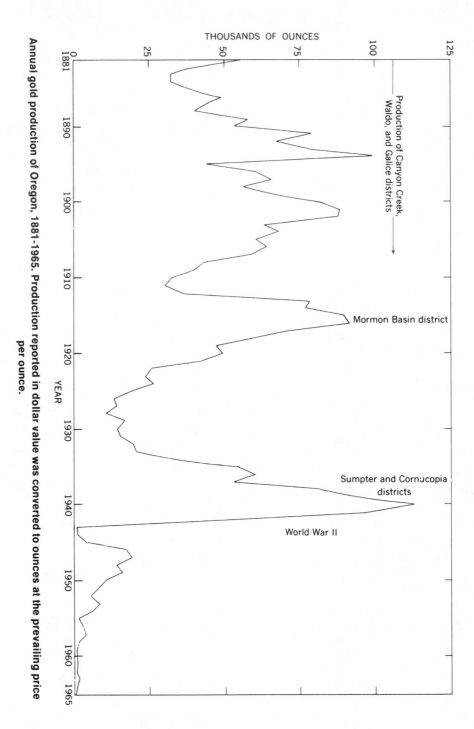

Annual gold production of Oregon, 1881-1965. Production reported in dollar value was converted to ounces at the prevailing price per ounce.

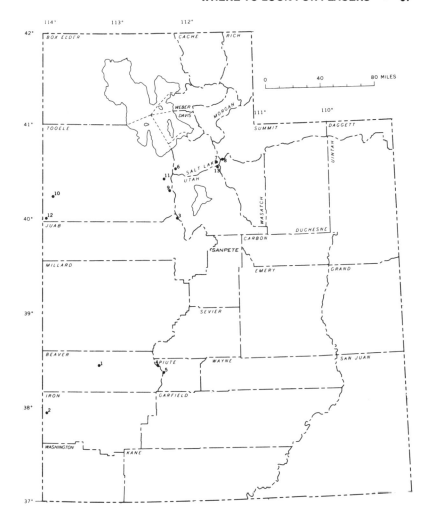

Gold-mining districts of Utah.

Beaver County:
.1, San Francisco.
Iron County:
2, Stateline.
Juab County:
3, Tintic.
Piute County:
4, Gold Mountain; 5, Mount Baldy.

Salt Lake County:
6, Cottonwood; 7, Bingham.
Summit and Wasatch Counties:
8, Park City.
Tooele County:
9, Camp Floyd; 10, Ophir-Rush Valley; 11, Clifton; 12, Willow Springs.
Utah County:
13, American Fork.

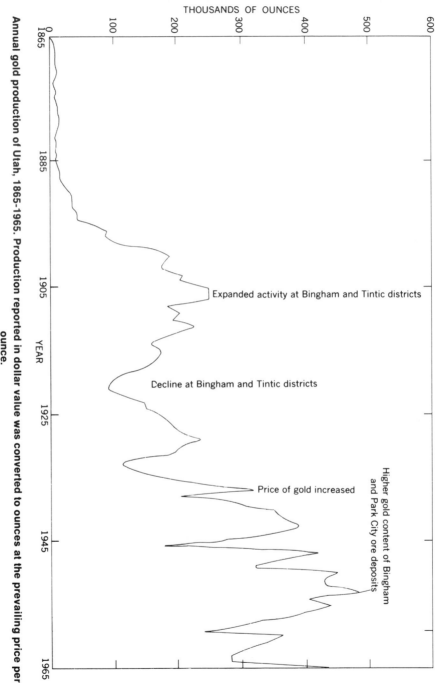

THOUSANDS OF OUNCES

Expanded activity at Bingham and Tintic districts

Decline at Bingham and Tintic districts

Price of gold increased

Higher gold content of Bingham and Park City ore deposits

YEAR

Annual gold production of Utah, 1865-1965. Production reported in dollar value was converted to ounces at the prevailing price per ounce.

Chelan County:
1, Blewett; 2, Entiat; 3, Chelan
Lake; 4, Wenatchee.

Ferry County:
5, Republic.

Kittitas County:
6, Swauk.

Okanogan County:
7, Cascade; 8, Methow; 9, Myers
Creek; 10, Oroville-Nightawk.

Snohomish County:
11, Monte Cristo; 12, Silverton.

Stevens County:
13, Orient.

Whatcom County:
14, Mount Baker; 15, Slate
Creek.

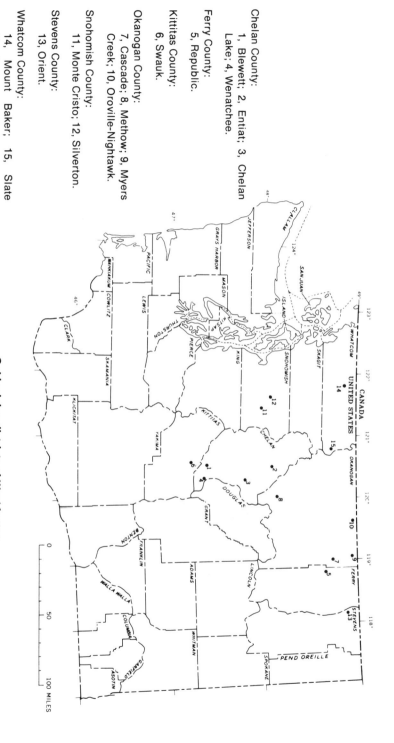

Gold-mining districts of Washington.

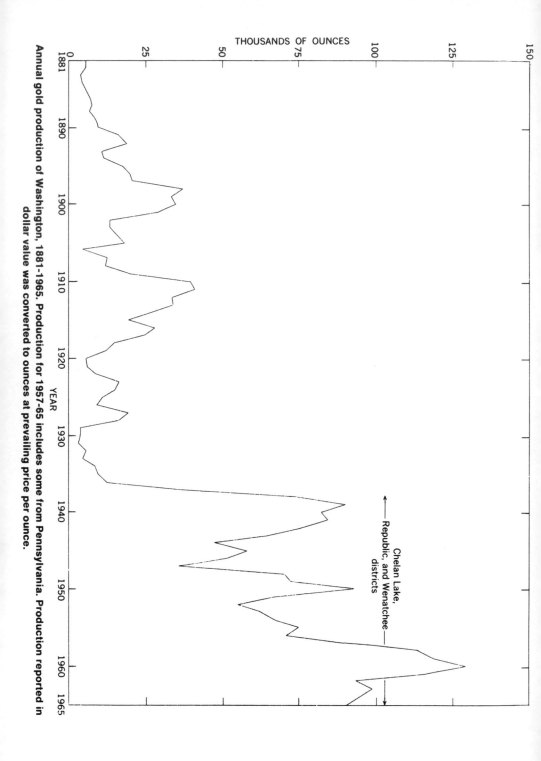

Annual gold production of Washington, 1881-1965. Production for 1957-65 includes some from Pennsylvania. Production reported in dollar value was converted to ounces at prevailing price per ounce.

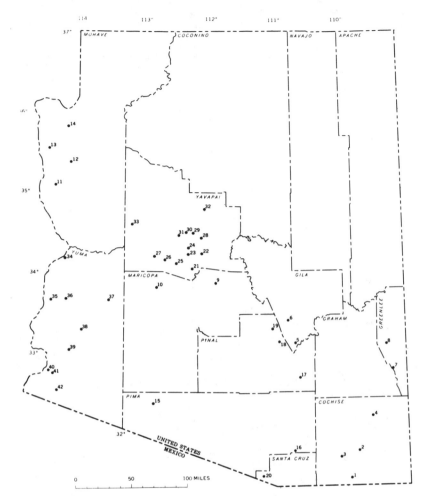

Gold-mining districts of Arizona.

Cochise County:
   1, Bisbee; 2, Turquoise; 3, Tomb-
stone; 4, Dos Cabezas.

Gila County:
   5, Banner; 6, Globe-Miami.

Greenlee County:
   7, Ash Peak; 8, Clifton-Morenci.

Maricopa County:
   9, Cave Creek; 10, Vulture.

Mohave County:
   11, San Francisco; 12, Wallapai;
13, Weaver; 14, Gold Basin.

Pima County:
   15, Ajo; 16, Greaterville.

Pinal County:
   17, Mammoth; 18, Ray; 19, Superior.

Santa Cruz County:
   20, Oro Blanco.

Yavapai County:
   21, Tiptop; 22, Black Canyon; 23,
Pine Grove-Tiger; 24, Peck; 25,
Black Rock; 26, Weaver-Rich
Hill; 27, Martineez; 28, Agua
Fria; 29, Big Bug; 30, Lynx
Creek-Walker; 31, Hassayampa-
Groom Creek; 32, Jerome; 33,
Eureka.

Yuma County:
   34, Cienega; 35, La Paz; 36,
Plomosa; 37, Ellsworth; 38, Kofa;
39, Castle Dome; 40, Laguna;
41, Dome; 42, Fortuna.

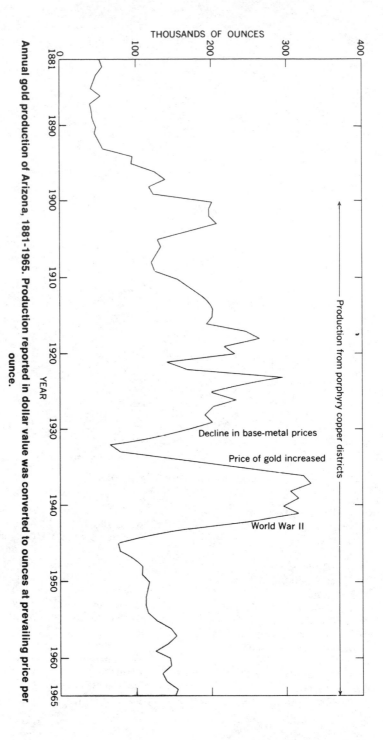

THOUSANDS OF OUNCES

Production from porphyry copper districts

Decline in base-metal prices

Price of gold increased

World War II

YEAR

Annual gold production of Arizona, 1881-1965. Production reported in dollar value was converted to ounces at prevailing price per ounce.

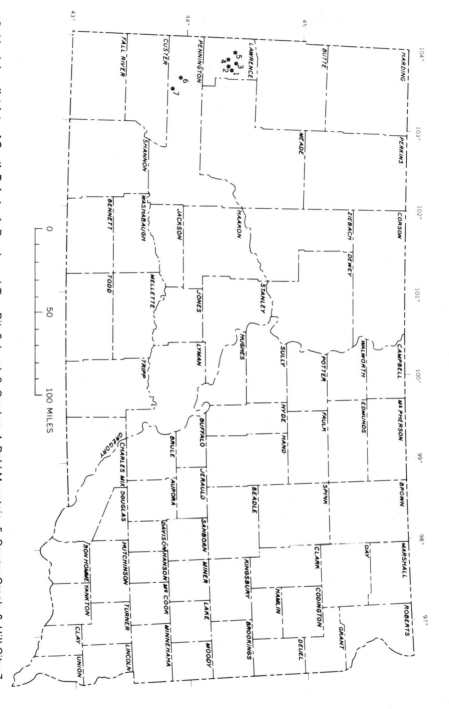

Gold-mining districts of South Dakota. 1, Deadwood-Two Bit; 2, Lead; 3, Garden; 4, Bald Mountain; 5, Squaw Creek; 6, Hill City; 7, Keystone.

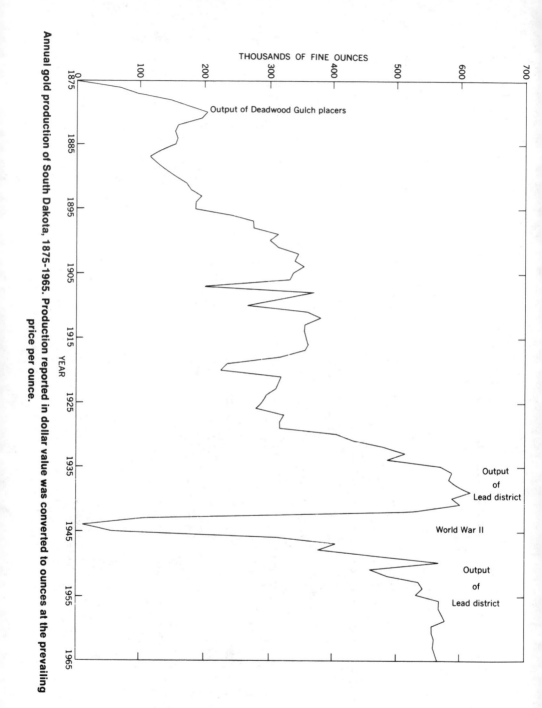

Annual gold production of South Dakota, 1875-1965. Production reported in dollar value was converted to ounces at the prevailing price per ounce.

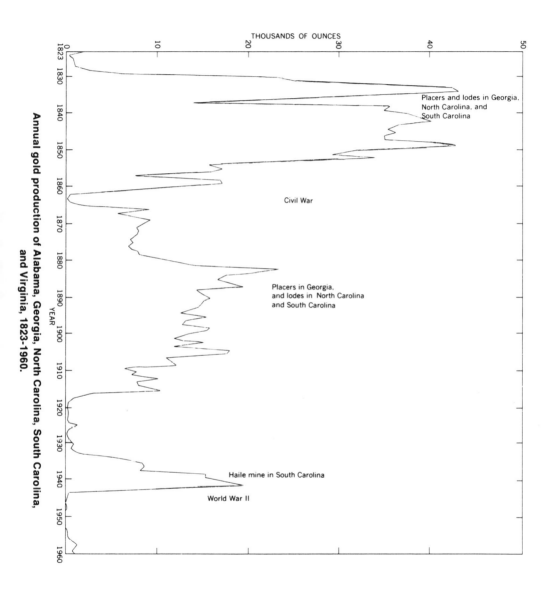

Annual gold production of Alabama, Georgia, North Carolina, South Carolina, and Virginia, 1823-1960.

THOUSANDS OF OUNCES

Placers and lodes in Georgia, North Carolina, and South Carolina

Civil War

Placers in Georgia, and lodes in North Carolina and South Carolina

Haile mine in South Carolina

World War II

YEAR

Chapter Five

PANNING GOLD

THE PYRAMIDS, ANCIENT though they are, are no older than the free and completely mobile art of panning gold. It is the method of both the poor man and the casual prospector of working promising ground, requiring no expensive equipment and little skill, although more aptitude is acquired the longer you try it. A frypan, burned free of grease in the campfire, will do the job. In fact, the great "Pike's Peak or Bust" gold rush was begun in 1859 when George Jackson panned some dirt in no more than an iron treaty cup, one of those handed to the Indians of the region by the Government.

The common gold pan in use today is a shallow circular utensil, with the sides sloping briefly out from the bottom, pressed from stiff sheet metal, usually lightweight steel or iron. In any event, the pan should be light for easy manipulation. Its smooth inner surface should definitely be kept free from grease and generally from rust, although some feel that a certain amount of rust and pitting helps catch the yellow metal.

The standard gold pan is 16 inches in diameter at the top and 2½ inches deep, the rim being flared outward at an angle of about 50° from the vertical. However, smaller 10-inch and 12-inch pans are more generally carried for testing. As a matter of fact, unless and until you settle into some long-term panning, it is suggested you use one of the widely available 12-inch pans. Again, before you use any kind of a receptacle for panning, it should be heated over a fire, or thoroughly scoured, until every last vestige of greasiness has disappeared.

The pan, as a matter of fact, need not even be metal. In the tropics a so-called *batea,* a wooden receptacle not unlike a large salad bowl, is used with considerable success, a skillful native being able to handle around 100 cubic feet of gravel with it in a day.

To start, fill your gold pan about half full of gravel and sand, most promisingly dug as close to bed rock as possible. With experience, you may come to prefer to fill the pan level with the top or even to round the load a bit. In any event, now submerge it in water—still water, six inches to a foot deep, being best.

Now knead the contents until all clay is dispersed and all lumps of dirt are thoroughly broken. If the water where you are working is shallow enough, set the pan on the bottom and work with both hands. Otherwise, hold the pan with one hand and work with the other. Pick out the larger stones and pebbles by hand, watching for nuggets. Throw the worthless pieces away.

Then the pan is held flat and shaken under water to allow the heavy gold to settle to the bottom. The pan is then tilted and raised quickly, still under water, so that a swirling motion washes off some of the lighter top material. Keep this up with a rotary motion, lowering first one wrist and then the other, occasionally shaking the pan under water or with water in it until only the gold and the other heavy minerals remain. Sharply tap the pan occasionally to help settle these.

With proper manipulation, this material concentrates at an edge of the bottom of the pan. Care must be taken that none of the gold climbs to the top of the pan or gets on top of the dirt. The process is repeated, slowing toward the end, until with the typical material nothing is left in the pan but black sand and gold.

Nuggets and coarse colors of gold can now be readily picked out with a tweezer or a knife point. Cleaning the black sand from the finer gold is more difficult. However, it can be carried nearly or entirely to completion by carefully swirling the contents as described above, always watching to make sure that none of the colors are climbing toward the lip. This part of the operation is commonly done

over another pan or in a tub so that if any gold is lost, it can be recovered by repanning.

The concentrates should be dried. The black sands, composed largely of magnetite (which is iron oxide), can then be removed with a magnet or by gently blowing them over a smooth flat surface. You can save time with the magnet, which may be of the ordinary horseshoe variety, by covering the ends with cellophane. Then once the cellophane is withdrawn, the magnetite will drop free. But, inasmuch as these grains are lighter than the gold, it is frequently possible to just blow them away.

In sampling work, particular care should be taken not to lose any of the fine colors. When actually mining, however, the additional time needed to insure that all the colors are saved very likely will not be justified because the value they add is so small.

THE PRINCIPLES OF PANNING

This method of separation, called panning, is based essentially on the principle that the heavier particles settle most rapidly from a mixture suspended in water. To say it another way, if a mixture of fragments is stirred up in water, the heavier particles will settle first.

Two factors determine which are the heavier particles; namely, size and specific gravity. Obviously, with two particles of identical material, the larger is the heavier. With two equal-sized particles of different material, the one with the higher specific gravity will be the heavier. The specific gravity of quartz, for example, is 2.6 and of the galena of our crystal-radio-set days 7.5. With a piece of quartz and one of galena equal in size, the galena would weigh approximately three times more than the quartz. It would also follow that with a chip of galena only one-third the size of a segment of quartz, both would weigh roughly the same.

The preceding rule holds except when particles are very tiny. Such minute bits tend to remain suspended irrespective of the kind of material and if sufficiently small, actually will remain in suspension. A number of factors other than the two mentioned, such as the shape of the particles, electric charges on them, density of suspension, etc. affect the settling rate. Inasmuch as panning is essentially a matter of making a suspension in water from which the valuable heavy materials settle out, the fact that minute bits of them tend to stay in suspension should be kept in mind in an effort to minimize losses from the pan.

Another way valuable heavy materials can be lost in panning is through the admixture of oily impurities. The ability of oil to cause such heavy minerals to float to the surface of a suspension is actually the basis of a process used in milling ores called floatation. Oil, being lighter than water, tends to rise to the surface, and small particles of heavy minerals coated with oil or attached to drops of oil are lifted with it. Particles so lifted could be washed out of the pan and lost, a reason for the burning of any oil out of a receptacle before it is used for panning.

The panning material is brought into suspension by causing water to move or flow around the pan, thereby providing a current with the power to carry particles in suspension. Everyone who has ever washed dishes is familiar with the fact that moving or flowing water can bring particles into suspension and hold them there so long as the speed at which the water is moving does not drop.

Everyone likely has removed material from a dish or pan of some kind by putting in water and causing the water to swirl around until all particles have been picked up, then pouring out the water. We know that if we stop causing the water to swirl, particles immediately begin settling. We also know that the heavier the particles are, the faster we have to make the water swirl to pick them up. The principle we are applying is simply: the load which moving water can carry depends on the speed or velocity with which it moves. Actually, this ratio is such that if the velocity is doubled, the transporting power is increased 64 times.

In panning, where the purpose is to retain certain material such as gold, the principle should be recognized and the current created by running water into or out of the pan kept at a low velocity so that heavy particles will not be brought into suspension and carried away.

OTHER MINERALS

You'll probably find other minerals in your gold pan, and this can be important in the long run because the subsequent operation of the workings to remove such additional metals as silver and platinum could greatly increase the value of the claim. This is one matter in which you may be able to use some expert advice.

In the meantime, you should be aware that pyrite (fool's gold, an iron sulphide) is often mistaken for gold by the novice. Pyrite, generally a brassy yellow to white in color, will shatter when struck with a hammer, unlike the malleable gold, and becomes a black powder when finely ground. Another trickster is mica which, distinguished by its light weight and its flat, platelike cleavage, may have a bright, bronzy appearance. Both minerals are common in gold regions.

Other minerals that will collect with the gold and black sands because of high specific gravity include ilmentite (an iron-black mineral composed of iron, titanium, and oxygen), hematite (non-magnetic iron oxide), marcasite (similar to pyrites but of a different crystalline organization), rutile (titanium oxide), wolframite (an iron manganese tungstate with a brownish or greyish black luster), scheelite (calcium tungstate), zircon (zirconium silicate), cinnabar (mercuric sulphide), chromite (chromium and iron oxides), and tourmaline (aluminum and boron silicate).

If present in sufficient quantity, these latter minerals may have economic significance. Native platinum, elemental quicksilver, and similar materials are also occasionally found in the pan.

AMALGAMATE

If there is an excessive amount of flour gold, such as you'll find when working such a stream as the Peace River where it flows by our cabin in northern British Columbia, a method of recovering the fine values is to place about a teaspoonful of quicksilver in the pan, then stir around the gold and the sands diligently with a stip of black iron so that the mercury makes contact with all the bits of gold and forms an amalgam. This can be separated from the other contents without any trouble.

It is not so simple to conserve the surplus quicksilver, some of which can be poured off and collected in another receptacle. A pellet or ball of amalgam resembles a smooth, lustrous golden nugget.

DO NOT EAT THE POTATO

A common, ordinary white potato can be used as a retort in recovering the gold from up to about an ounce of amalgam. You'll need a large, reasonably round potato which, fresh and moist, has not begun to dry out and crack. Cut this in half.

Scoop out of the middle of the two halves, or the center of the larger half, a hole big enough to contain the amalgam. When this latter is in position, wire the two halves of the potato together.

Bake until done, only outdoors where there is good air circulation. In a 450° camp oven this will take about an hour, the potato being ready when you can pick it up in a folded towel, press it, and find it soft within. Where you'll most likely be carrying on the operation, though, will be in the campfire. Get a good hardwood fire going and bury the potato in hot ashes, not glowing coals, for about an hour. Pretty well blackened on the outside, it'll be done when a thin, sharpened stick will press through it easily.

Then rack it out and allow it to cool. Unwire the potato and secure what will now be a small gold button in its interior. Put the potato in a dish and squeeze out the distilled mercury for use again. Discard the poisonous remains where neither your dog, not anything else, will make the mistake of eating it.

Be warned, too, that the fumes of volatized quicksilver are poisonous in the extreme.

WHEN TO PAN

In most cases, unless you're traveling very light, you'll use your pan only to determine the presence of gold and will not continue panning with the object of actually recovering significant amounts of the mineral. As we'll consider in a moment, there are easier ways to do this.

But you should regard panning as your best means of determining the presence of heavy metals, therefore ordinarily pan first in preference to looking at material with a hand lens. You should pan anything showing signs of mineralization; that is, most commonly rust or quartz. In the case of rust, a full pan of fine rusty material can generally be scraped up without too much difficulty.

If the rusty material is solid, however, a sample must be selected to grind in a mortar before panning. Quartz must also be ground in a mortar before panning. In such cases, the amount of material panned should be largely governed by the length of time required to pulverize it. If the material is difficult to break up, as will be the case with quartz, a selection of small pieces of the best looking material should be made. You'll be able to grind these in a very short time, and they'll probably be enough to tell the story.

HOW FINE TO GRIND

The purpose of grinding is to liberate any particles of gold and other valuable elements from the minerals enclosing them. Ideally the grind should be fine enough to accomplish this. All you will be able to do, however, is to pulverize to a reasonable degree of fineness.

Coarse particles can be ground down comparatively easily until they'll pass through a 60 mesh screen, but the grinding becomes increasingly difficult with each succeeding reduction in size. It is good practice, incidentally, to use a small screen when grinding material for panning, as this assures a certain degree of fineness which might not otherwise be achieved. Too, the maximum size of the bits stays small, also helpful in panning the sample.

A good screen can be made by soldering a piece of 60 or 80 mesh screen onto a small tin can which has had its ends smoothly removed.

TAILING UP

When the concentrate has been obtained, it must be minutely examined. The tried and tested method is to put a small amount of water in the pan, then tilt or rock the pan gently so that the fluid runs over the concentrate in the angle between the side and bottom of the receptacle, carrying the lighter particles to the end of the concentrate. This is continued until all the lighter bits have been moved along, leaving the heaviest, as for example the gold, in a "tail" or "colors" at the head of the concentrate.

Fortunately in the case of gold, if a considerable number of colors are present in the tail, this can be seen easily. But whether a tail can be seen or not, the concentrate should be closely examined with a hand lens. In fact, if only a few very small gold particles are present, they may not be seen without the aid of a hand lens. By the way, such particles when moved along by the water have a characteristic, slow rolling action which is helpful in identifying them.

ROASTING

You'll find that in many of your pannings, a fairly large concentrate of sulphides will be obtained. Since these particles may be as heavy as fine bits of gold, they make it difficult to tail out the gold. You cannot be sure exactly how much gold is present or, in some cases, if there is any gold at all. But there's a trick of the trade.

The sulphides can be eliminated by roasting, also called burning. It is sound practice to roast whenever a large concentrate of sulphides is obtained, another important reason being that fine particles of gold are commonly locked up in the larger sulphide pieces, and these must be broken up if the gold is to be liberated.

The handiest technique is to dry the concentrate obtained by panning, then to place it on a tin lid such as that from a coffee can. Set this lid carefully on a hot fire. The sulphides will then commence to burn. Continue until no more sulphur or arsenic fumes come off.

Then remove the lid from the fire and allow it to cool. The rusty cake remaining should be put in the mortar and ground to a fine powder. Transfer this to the gold pan, gently wash it, and then examine it as in the just described method of tailing up. If appreciable amounts of sulphides still remain, the roasting process should be repeated.

If you are in country where there are a lot of sulphides, you may prepare yourself for this process by bringing along some inexpensive potassium chlorate, Mix this with the sulphides before heating. When warmth is then applied, the chlorate will decompose, furnishing oxygen which will markedly hasten the burning of the sulphides, assuring a more complete roast.

ESTIMATION OF GRADE FROM PANNING

The size or length of a tail of colors in the gold pan can be the basis for estimating the gold content of a sample, although accuracy comes with practice. The generally pursued method is to pan carefully a known quantity of ore, roasting if necessary, to obtain a tail of colors. The number of colors are counted, extra allowances being made for the larger ones.

A sample of identical material is taken and its actual grade determined by assay. This way, a ratio is established between the number of colors and the actual richness of the find. The number of colors corresponding to other grades can likewise be established by panning and assaying.

The same amount of material should be used in all testing. Then the grade of other samples can be estimated by counting the colors of the tails and comparing them with the ratios already established. However, it should be noted that so many variable factors are involved that such estimates cannot be relied on too heavily. Moremover, most gold occurrences appear to have their own characteristics, and even if a satisfactory basis for estimating is worked out for one, the chances are that it will not hold for another.

Chapter Six

OTHER METHODS OF GETTING GOLD

AT LEAST TWICE as much gravel can be worked per day with a rocker than with a pan. The rocker or cradle, as it is sometimes called, must still be manipulated carefully to prevent the loss of fine gold. But with it the manual labor of washing is less strenuous although the same method, perhaps shovel and pick, is used for excavating the gravel.

The rocker, like the gold pan, is extensively used in small-scale placer work, both for sampling and for washing sluice concentrates and material cleaned by hand from bedrock. One to three cubic yards, bank measure, can be dug and washed in a rocker per man-shift, depending on the distance the gravel or water has to be carried, the character of the gravel, and the size of the rocker.

On the other hand, an experienced individual can wash about 10 large pans per hour, the equivalent of approximately one-half to one cubic yard of gravel a day, depending on how clean the gravel is. A standard 16-inch pan, filled level, might contain roughly 22 pounds of dry bank gravel. There are roughly 150 to 180 such pans per cubic yard. More than twice as many 12-inch pans would be required per cubic yard. In any event, the top dirt or cover is usually cast aside and the first few inches of material directly above bedrock, as well as the material scraped from crevices, worked.

Rockers are generally homemade and display a variety of designs. One favorite, which is illustrated, consists essentially of a combination washing box and screen, a canvas or carpet apron under the screen, a short sluice with one or more riffles, and rockers under the sluice.

The bottom of the washing box consists of sheet metal with holes about one-half inch in diameter punched in it. Or use a one-inch-mesh screen. Dimensions shown are satisfactory, but variations are certainly possible, depending on the job at hand and on the materials available. However, the bottom of the rocker should be made of a single, wide, smooth board, as this will greatly facilitate cleanups. The materials for building a rocker cost only a few dollars, depending mainly upon the source of lumber.

The gravel, after being dampened, is placed in the box, one or two shovelfuls at a time. Water is then poured on the gravel while the rocker is swayed back and forth. You can dip up the water with a simple long-handled utensil made by nailing a tin can to the end of a stick. If available, a small stream from a pipe or hose will be even better.

The gravel is washed clean in the box. After being inspected for nuggets, the oversize material is dumped out. The undersize substances go over the apron, where most of the gold is caught. Care should be taken, however, that too much water is not poured on at once, as then some of the gold may be flushed out. The riffles are there to stop any gold that gets over the apron.

In regular mining work, the rocker is cleaned up after every two to three hours; oftener when rich ground is being worked and the yellow metal begins showing early on the apron and in the riffles. In cleaning up after a run, water is poured through while the washer is gently rocked, and the surface sand and dirt are washed from the top. Then the apron is turned into a pan.

The material back of the riffles in the sluice is taken up with a flat scoop, placed at the head of the sluice, and washed down gently once or twice with clear water. The gold remains behind on the boards, from which it is scraped up and put into the pan with the concentrates from the apron. The few colors left in the sluice will be caught with the next run. The concentrate is now cleaned in the pen.

Skillful manipulation of the rocker and careful cleanups permit recovery of nearly all the gold. Violent rocking should be avoided. Otherwise, the gold may splash out of the apron or over the riffles. The sand behind the riffles should be stirred occasionally, especially if it shows a tendency to pack hard, to prevent loss of gold. If there is much clay in the gravel, it may be necessary to soak it for some hours in a tub of water before rocking it.

Where water is scarce, two small reservoirs are constructed, one in front and the other to the rear of the rocker. The reservoir at the front serves as a settling basin. The overflow drains back to the one at the rear, and the water is used over again.

The capacity of rockers can be increased by using power drives. Such a device might be rocked by an eccentric arm at the rate of approximately 40 six-inch strokes per minute. The capacity of the typical machine with two men working will then be about a cubic yard per hour. When the gravel is free of clay, however, the capacity may be as great as three cubic yards an hour. The cost of a mechanized rocker and a secondhand engine for driving it is estimated at $450.

DIP BOX

The so-called dip box is useful where water is scarce and where an ordinary sluice cannot be used because of the terrain. It is not only portable, but it will handle about the same quantity of material as the rocker.

Construction is relatively simple. The box has a bottom of one-by-12-inch lumber to which are nailed one-by-six-inch sides and an end that serves as the back or head. At the other end is nailed a piece approximately one-inch high.

The bottom of the box is covered with burlap, canvas, or thin carpet to catch the gold. Over this, starting one foot below the back end of the box, is nailed a one-by-three-foot strip of heavy wire screen of about one-quarter-inch mesh. The fabric and screen are held in place by cleats along the sides of the box. Overall length may be six to eight feet, although nearly all the gold will likely be collected in the first three feet.

The box is placed so that the back is about waist high, the other end being one-half to one foot lower. Material is simply dumped or shoveled into the upper end and washed by pouring water over it from a dipper, bucket, hose, or pipe until it passes through the box. The water should not be run through so hard that it washes the gold away. Larger stones, after being washed, are thrown out by hand, or a screen box can be added to separate them. Riffles can be added to the lower section of the box if it is believed gold is being lost.

THE ROCKER

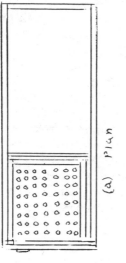

(a) Plan

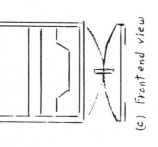

Handle

Apron

Baffle

grizzly box

grizzle

1"x2" stop support for grizzly box

bulkhead

2" curved strap iron

12   1½

center pin (loose)

2" cradle support

(b) Cutaway Elevation

(c) Front end view

Notes: All lumber with the exception of the cradle supports, is 1-inch dressed material.

Apron consists of a frame covered with canvas slack enough to form a slight belly. Apron slope is 1-1/2" per foot.

Center pins should be loose enough to allow a free rocking movement.

Grizzly holes are 1/2 inch in diameter.

The operation of the here-illustrated rocker consists of shoveling gravel onto a screen or grizzly, pouring water over it from a dipper, and at the same time giving the device a rocking motion. The grizzly retains all the stones, which are removed when washed clean. The water and the undersize pass onto a canvas apron which saves most of the gold and places the remainder at the head end of the trough.

Riffles, canvas, blankets, corduroy, burlap, or cocoa matting with expanded metal have been used to cover the bottom of the trough with varying degrees of success in saving the gold. The combination of cocoa matting covered with expanded metal lath has proved to be quite effective for most gravels. The frequency of the cleaning up depends on the richness and character of the gravel.

The rocking motion should be sufficient to keep the gravel disturbed, allowing the gold to settle out, but a too vigorous movement will cause a gold loss. The gravel bed should be lifted slightly with each motion and should be evenly distributed across the trough. Generally speaking, the rocker is not noted for its ability to save fine gold, but with careful and expert manipulation high recoveries can be achieved. Tailings from rockers and sluice boxes should be occasionally panned to check for gold losses. When gold is found near the lower end of the rocker or sluice box, losses should be suspected.

BASIC DESIGN FOR A PROSPECTOR'S ROCKER

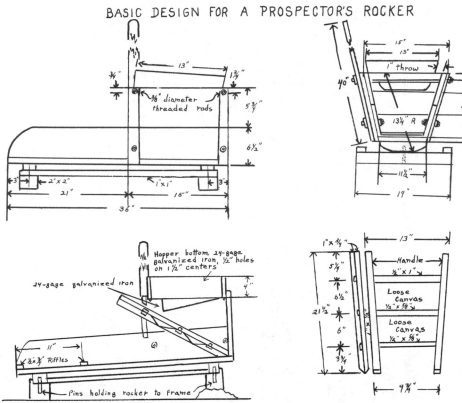

Note that hopper is built to slide back and forth, bumping the sides as unit is rocked.

Rockers are usually homemade and display a variety of designs. A favorite design, as illustrated, consists essentially of a combination washing box and screen, a canvas or carpet apron under the screen, a short sluice with two or more riffles, and rockers under the sluice.

The bottom of the washing box consists of sheet metal with holes about ½ inch in diameter punched in it, or a ½-inch-mesh screen can be used. Dimensions shown are satisfactory, but variations are possible. The bottom of the rocker should be made of a single, wide, smooth board, which will greatly facilitate cleanups. The materials for building a rocker cost only a few dollars, depending mainly upon the source of lumber.

LONG TOM

A Long Tom usually has a greater capacity than a rocker and, more important, does not require the labor of rocking. It consists essentially of a short receiving launder, an open washing box six to 12 feet long, with the lower end a perforated plate or a screen set at an angle, and a short sluice with riffles, as illustrated. The component boxes are set on slopes ranging from one to one-and-one-half inches per foot. The drop between boxes aids in breaking lumps of clay, thus freeing any contained gold.

A good supply of water is needed for the successful operation of a Long Tom. This water is introduced into the receiving box with the gravel, from where both pass into the washing box. The sand, small gravel, and water pass through the screen's half-inch openings and into the sluice. The oversize material is forked out. The gold, thus, is caught by the riffles. The concentrates here are removed, when they accumulate sufficiently, and recleaned in a pan. Mercury can be used in the riffles if the substances contain much fine gold.

The quantity of gravel that can be treated per day will vary with the nature of the gravel, the water supply, and the number of men employed to shovel into the Tom and to fork out the larger stones. For example, two men, one shoveling into the Tom and the other working on it, might wash six cubic yards of ordinary gravel, or three to four yards of cemented gravel, in 10 hours.

A Tom can be operated by a crew of four men; two shoveling in, one forking out the stones, and the fourth shoving away the fine tailings.

SLUICE

When running water and a grade are available, a simple sluice is ordinarily as effective as a Long Tom and requires less labor. A sluice is generally described as an artificial channel through which controlled amounts of water flow. The important aspect is that sluicing throughout the world had produced by far the largest proportion of placer gold.

Some initial expense is involved for the building of the sluice boxes and the setting up of a controlled water supply, plus the basic work in readying the ground for economic operation. The job usually needs the efforts of more than one man. On the other hand, it provides for working far greater yardages a day than do hand methods. Therefore, lower grades of gravel can be profitably handled than would be pos-

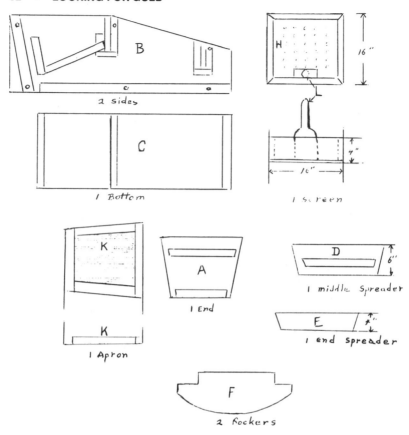

ROCKER PARTS

A - End, one piece 1″ x 14″, 16″ long.
B - Sides, two pieces 1″ x 14″, 48″ long.
C - Bottom, one piece 1″ x 14″, 44″ long.
D - Middle spreader, one piece 1″ x 6″, 16″ long.
E - End spreader, one piece 1″ x 4″, 15″ long.
F - Rockers, two pieces 2″ x 5″, 17″ long.
H - Screen, about 16″ square outside dimensions with screen bottom. Four pieces of 1″ x 4″, 15½″ long and one piece of screen 16″ square with ¼″ or ½″ openings or sheet metal perforated with similar size round openings.

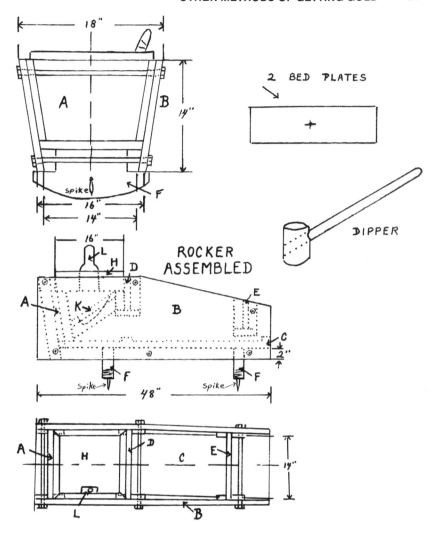

K - Apron, made of 1″ x 2″ stubs covered loosely with canvas. For cleats and apron, etc., 27 feet of 1″ x 2″ are needed. Six pieces of ⅜″ iron rod 19″ long, threaded 2″ on each end and fitted with nuts and washes.

L - The handle in the drawing is fitted on the screen, where it helps to lift the screen from the body. Some prefer it fastened to the body.

In the center of each rocker is a spike that fits into holes bored into the planks on which the rocker stands, to prevent slipping. Riffles should be made so they can be easily removed for cleaning up. A dipper made of a tomato can with perforated bottom and 30-inch handle is also necessary for adding water.

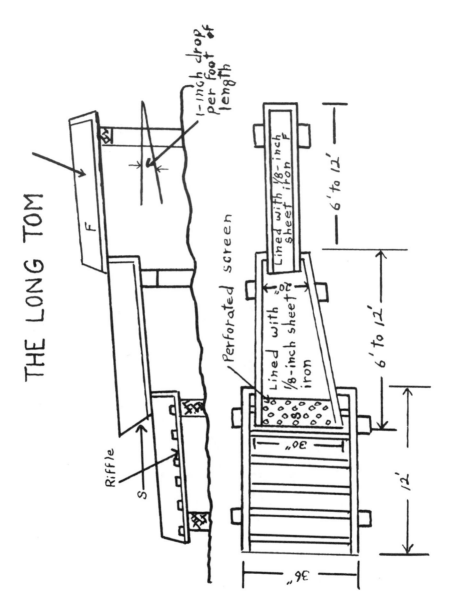

THE LONG TOM

F

1-inch drop per foot of length

Perforated screen

Riffle

S

Lined with ⅛-inch sheet iron F

Lined with ⅛-inch sheet iron

6' to 12'

6' to 12'

12'

30"

36"

Note: Some Long Toms or flumes may be 40, 50, or 80 feet long, all riffled and lined with burlap or carpeting. Thus, bank-run dirt can be shoveled in at any point. When stream water is diverted to the box, the system is commonly called fluming and is frequently used in clandestine placering to avoid engine noise.

sible with pan or rocker. Furthermore, the running water provides much of the work that otherwise would have to be undertaken by hand. Finally, adequately made sluice boxes will catch all the fine, rusty, and flour gold that can be economically saved.

Before you go to the time and expense of putting in a sluice, though, you should make reasonably sure of two factors. There should be enough sufficiently rich gravel to justify the expenditure. An important part of any sluicing operation, too, is its water supply, and where water is not sufficiently plentiful, pumps, pipelines, or even dams with special head gates may be required.

In the majority of instances a slant of six inches for a 12-foot box is adequate for the average ground to be worked. However, this need may build up to 10 to 12 inches per box for clay which will need a heavy grade for its disintegration. This will be true, likewise, for cemented gravels which, additionally, will likely require several short falls along the line of sluice boxes if they are to be broken up. If the grade of the bedrock in the slope itself is too little to allow sufficient drop for sluicing, you can either resort to trenching or to raising the lead boxes on trestles.

Incidentally, when you need new sluice boxes, the old ones should be burned and the ashes panned.

Small-scale sluicing by hand methods has been appropriately called shoveling-into-boxes. In contrast, in the usually more efficient operation of ground sluicing, most of the excavation is accomplished by the action of water flowing openly over the materials to be mined. In both cases, the materials pass through a sluice where the gold is collected behind riffles. A variation of the sluicing technique, where water is stored and intermittently released against or across the materials, is called "booming."

A sluiceway in its simplest form may be a 12-foot-long plank of one-by12-inch lumber to which sides some 10 to 12 inches high are nailed, these latter being secured by braces at several places across the top. Larger boxes can be made, with battens added to cover the joints between boards where gold might otherwise slip out and with braces built around the outsides of the box for greater rigidity.

To provide for a series of boxes, the ends should be beveled or the units tapered so that one will slip into the other in descending order and form tight joints. Four to eight such boxes in sequence would be a typical installation.

Two men shoveling by hand into sluice boxes can wash five to 10 times as much gravel as could be put through a rocker in a day. The slope of the sluice and the supply of water must be adjusted so the

Sluices
Scale ½" = 1'

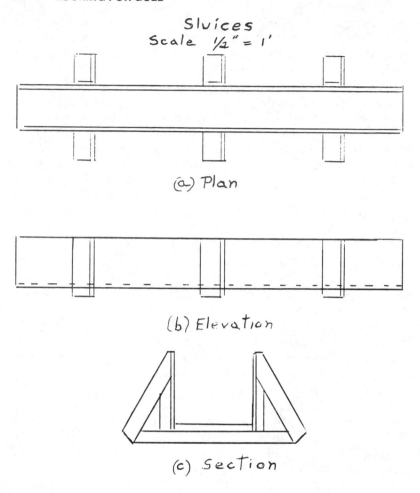

(a) Plan

(b) Elevation

(c) Section

Here is a small sluice, one suitable for prospecting or for a small-scale hand operation. A sluice of this type is easily built and fairly inexpensive. On the other hand, it will have a relatively short life compared to boxes of sturdier construction. Although not shown in the drawing, sluices of this type may be made to telescope; for instance, one end may be 14" wide and the other 12". This allows a longer sluice to be erected and transported with a minimum of time and labor. Canvas is usually placed at the joint to prevent leakage. Long sluices may also be made by merely butting two or more boxes together and fastening them by means of an overlapping sleeve, canvas again being used to seal the joint.

gravel, including larger stones, will keep moving through the boxes and on out. Slopes of four to 12 inches per 12-foot box are normal, but if water is in short supply, the slope may be increased. Trestles may be necessary to support the boxes over excavated ground, gullies, or marshy depressions.

Various kinds of riffles may be employed within the boxes, depending upon the availabilities of materials and personal preference. The riffles, which go on the bottom, are generally set crosswise in the box, but they can also be effective when laid lengthwise, as for instance a flooring of straight round poles, the concentrates settling between them. Riffles may be of wood or of angle or strap iron, or a combination. A pattern of square blocks or stones can serve as riffles. Rubber or plastic strips have been used. Durability is important for prolonged operations, so wood can be armored with metal. Heavy wire screen, expended metal, or cocoa mats make good riffles for collecting fine gold.

A common height for riffles is 1½ inches. They can be placed from one-half to several inches apart. Fastening the riffles to a rack, which is then wedged in place in the sluiceway, permits their easy removal. A tapered shape on the cross riffle, with the thinner edge to the bottom, tends to set up an eddying action that is favorable for concentration. Another way to achieve this eddying action is to cant the riffle or merely just its top.

Burlap or blanket material is commonly placed under the riffles to help in collecting fine gold. Quicksilver can be added to some sections of the sluice if there is much fine gold, but care must be taken to prevent escape of this mercury.

Sluice cleanups should be made at fairly regular intervals. After running clear water until the sluiceway is free of gravel, riffles are removed in sections beginning at the upper end. With a thin stream of water, the lighter of the remaining material is washed to the sections below. The gold, heavy sands, and amalgam if mercury has been used are scraped up and placed in buckets. This mixture can then be panned or cleaned up in a rocker to obtain a final concentrate or amalgam.

FEEDING THE SLUICE

When feeding the sluice, it is common in a small operation to place closely spaced bars of some sort or a heavy screen across the section where the gravels enter, to eliminate the larger stones which are probably worthless, anyway. The bars, known as a grizzly, or the screen

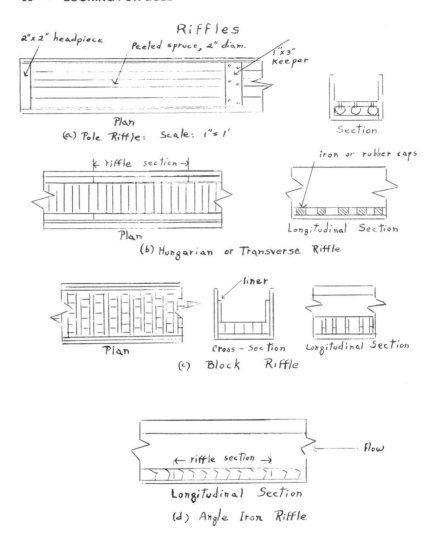

Riffles

2"x 2" headpiece

Peeled spruce, 2" diam.

1"x3" keeper

Plan

Section

(a) Pole Riffle: Scale: 1"= 1'

← riffle section →

iron or rubber caps

Plan

Longitudinal Section

(b) Hungarian or Transverse Riffle

liner

Plan

Cross - Section

Longitudinal Section

(c) Block Riffle

Flow

← riffle section →

Longitudinal Section

(d) Angle Iron Riffle

The actual gold saving devices are riffles which are placed in the bottom of the sluices. Their function is to break up the material passing over them — slowing it down to allow the denser particles to settle out, to form pockets to retain gold as it settles, and to form eddies or boils which roughly classify the material in the riffle spaces. The riffle shape, spacing, and position with respect to the flow determine the boil, which should be strong enough to prevent the riffles from packing but still allow deposition of gold.

The choice of riffles for an operation depends largely on the size of the gold in the deposit. Figure (a) shows a type of pole riffle which has proved successful as a saver of coarse gold. As it does not retard the current as much as other types, more yardage with less water can be treated in a given period of time, but for the same reason it is a poor recoverer of fine gold. In some operations, the pole riffle (general term: longitudinal riffle) is replaced with iron rails, which offer longer service. Longitudinal riffles are often placed in the head end of boxes and are followed by Hungarian riffles.

Figure (b) shows a Hungarian or transverse riffle, probably the most widely used type in all sluicing operations. This riffle gives more resistance to flow and is a better collector of fine gold. The riffle spacing tends to pack, however, especially when heavy black sands are present in large quantity. When this happens, frequent cleanups become necessary. As shown, riffles are usually made in sections to provide ease in handling during cleanups. In addition, they are often capped with strips of iron or rubber to prolong their life.

A variation of the Hungarian riffle is the block riffle, fig. (c). Used often in the upper portion of the sluice, they are economical when timber is cheap. They are easily replaced and give a smooth floor over which boulders may slide; they wear quickly, however, when placed under heavy service. Also shown in this drawing are sluice liners or sideplates. They are almost always used in all kinds of sluices and serve the double function of preventing wear on the sides of the sluice and holding the riffles in place. However, for the small wooden prospecting sluice, the life of the box itself would probably not justify their use, and the riffle hold-downs are nailed in place through the sides of the sluice.

Another variation of the Hungarian riffle is the angle-iron riffle shown in figure (d). These are usually placed in sluices made of steel plate. Steel sluice boxes have a life measured in seasons and, if much mining is to be done in one general area, are well worth their high capital investment. As shown in the figure, the angle-irons are made up in sections by welding the ends of a narrow plate, placing the riffles at a slight angle to encourage a more vigorous riffle boil. The dimensions and spacing are not rigid, as is the case in all the drawings, but may be varied to suit the individual operator and the conditions imposed by the deposit.

When in place, the sluice box should be perfectly level across its width and have firm support and constant grade throughout its length.

Although usually placed on the ground, sluices are sometimes elevated on trestles to attain grade and / or to provide space for tailings. Grades have varied from ½" to 1½" drop per foot of length. Too steep a grade will carry values out of the box, yet it should be enough so that the water will wash the material through unaided. In Interior Alaska, the average grade used is around 1½"/ft. The depth of water should be sufficient to move all but the largest rocks, but should not be greater than one-half the box width.

Gold recovery is hard to determine due to the difficulty of accurately sampling the sluice feed and tailings. Generally, the distribution of gold in the riffles is used as an indication. For instance, roughly 80% of the gold recovered should be in the first few feet of riffles, and if gold in significant amounts is found near the tail of the sluice, either the riffle arrangement or the grade needs altering. The amount of water, the slope of the boxes, the type and spacing of the riffles, all affect the gold recovery, packing of the riffles, etc. Determining the most efficient combination of factors is a matter of experimentation for each different deposit.

should be slanted so that oversize material rolls off to the side. The spacing, depending on the gradation of the feed, will generally be between one-quarter to one inch, three-eighths of an inch being a common size.

In larger operations, a rotating screen, or trommel, is often used. In a ground-sluicing operation possibly all materials will be run through the sluice boxes. Provisions must be made for removing the oversize materials, though, and if necessary to stack them away from the working area.

When the gravel contains much clay it may well be desirable to use a puddling box at the head of the string of sluice boxes. This may be any convenient size; say, six feet long by three feet wide, with six to eight-inch sides. The clayey material is shoveled into this box and broken up with a hoe or rake before being allowed to pass into the sluiceway. There is a double importance to this step. Not only may the lumps contain gold, but if they are allowed through the sluice, they can pick up and carry away gold particles already deposited.

After the boxes are set, shoveling starts at an advantageous point. Experienced miners work out the ground in regular cuts and in an orderly fashion. Enough faces are opened so that the shovelers will not interfere with one another. Provision is made to keep the bedrock cleaned. Boulders and stumps are moved a minimum number of times. Traverses are made of such widths and lengths that shoveling is made as easy as possible.

The boxes are kept as low as possible so that a minimum lift of gravel is necessary. At the same time, of course, an adequate slope must be maintained for the gravel to run through the boxes under the limitations of the available water. Leaks in the sluice are promptly stopped. Shoveling is done in such a manner that the sluice does not become clogged, nor does the water splash out too heavily and hamper shoveling. Allowance for dump room must be continuously provided at the end of the sluice. The best procedure, when possible of course, is to scatter the waste into a rapidly moving stream.

All material of a size that will run through the sluiceway is shoveled in, and the oversize stuff is thrown to one side. Boulders from the first cut should be stacked outside the workings, on barren ground if possible so they won't have to be handled again. When shoveling is from more than several feet away, it is best to set boards above and on the opposite side of the box to increase the efficiency of the shovelers. The greatest box height into which the average man can shovel is seven to eight feet, while if anything is above even five or six feet, the worker's efficiency is markedly reduced.

If the gravel is over three or four feet deep, it is usually excavated in benches to facilitate digging and to permit the upper layers to be raised a minimum shoveling height. When the gravel is shallow, wheelbarrows may be used. Another way is to shovel onto a conveyor belt that discharges into a trommel, discarding the oversize material and working the undersize substances through the sluice.

When two or more individuals are working in the same cut, the height of the succeeding benches is governed by the character of the material being dug and the distance the gravel has to be lifted. Excitement helps, too. On many placer diggings, it is the deep gravel that is rich.

The sluice may be maintained on the surface of unworked ground or supported on bents on the opposite side of the cut. After the first cut, the boxes are supported on bents as the ground underneath them is dug out. At other places the boxes may be set on bedrock and dirt shoveled into the head of the sluice from short transverse cuts at the upper end of the pit.

Work usually begins at the lower end of a deposit so that the bedrock can be kept drained, then proceeds across the deposit by regular cuts. The length and order of these cuts will depend on local conditions. As heavy sands and gravel build up deposits between the riffles in the sluice, it may be necessary to stir these to prevent packing and the consequent override of gold particles. A tined implement such as a pitchfork is often convenient for this. Large stones that lodge in the sluiceway can be similarly removed.

WHAT ABOUT WATER?

The quantity of available water will influence both the scale of operations and the size of the sluiceway used. A minimum flow of 15 to 20 miner's inches is required for a 12-inch-wide sluiceway with a steep grade.

One cubic foot of water equals 7½ gallons. One miner's inch equals 1½ cubic feet per minute or 11¼ gallons per minute. Forty miner's inches comes to one cubic foot per second.

You can still get by with smaller flows by storing the water in some sort of reservoir, then using the supply intermittently. A common practice, followed where the amount of water is limited, is to use a grizzly or screen over the sluice to eliminate oversize material and thus concentrate the water action on what's left. Reduction in the amount of material to be treated, by first running it through a trommel to wash and screen out the coarse size, is another effective method of lowering the water requirements.

Water is usually conducted via ditch to the sluice. However, if the ground is rich enough, it may be practicable to pump water for the sluice. The feasibility of obtaining a gravity flow should first be investigated, though, as the expense of pumping may be more than the cost of a long ditch when the cost is distributed over the yardage of gravel eventually to be moved. A suitable number of sluiceways, or some other removal system, may be used to transport the tailings to a dumping ground away from the working area. A tailings or settling pond may be required to maintain downstream water quality.

Ground sluicing utilizes the cascading effect of water to break down the gravel. Hence, the water requirements for this are much more critical. The chief application of ground sluicing is to run a stream bed through the deposits.

Pipelines, flumes, or ditches are necessary when ground sluicing is applied to gravels higher up on banks or terraces. The larger scale hydraulic methods would then become favorable. If booming is to be done, a dam and reservoir will be needed. The dam is usually equipped with a gate mechanism that permits either automatic or manual control and quick release of the impounded water for maximum washing effect. The water can be passed over the upper face of a gravel bank or diverted against the bottom to undercut and carry away the gravel as the face of the bank breaks down. All materials are channeled toward the sluice. In other words, the possibilities are unlimited.

The natural flow of a stream can be used by diverting the current with boards or simply with piled boulders. So-called shears can be constructed of one or two-inch-thick planks 12 feet long, nailed to pairs of tripods so that the planks slant back from the water flow at an angle of about 60°. The tripods are built in such a way that boulders can be piled inside the base to hold them in place. A row of such shears can be used to divert the force of the water against a bank, or two rows can be employed to form a flume.

The seasonal nature of stream flow in different areas must be kept in mind when planning any placer operation. State and Federal agencies may provide information on the water runoff of the larger streams, indicating limitations that may be expected due to seasonal changes.

HANDLING BOULDERS

Boulders are best left in place if it is at all possible to work around them. Sometimes, particularly in sluicing, it will become necessary to move boulders out of the way. Pole pries may do the job, or you may even need a derrick operated by a hand winch, steam, gasoline, or electrical power. Possibly several such derricks will be needed if many boulders are present.

Boulders may also be drilled with a jackhammer and blasted with dynamite. Or they may more simply be blasted with an explosive plastered on the rock, a technique called mud capping.

Sections of the pit where bedrock has been cleaned up may be reserved for stacking large rocks. Future operations, in any event, should be planned so repeated handling is avoided.

CLEANING BEDROCK

Cleanup of the last remaining materials from bedrock is an important stage in gold placering, and if the surface if soft, fractured, or uneven, this can become a painstaking chore. Where bedrock is soft and broken, gold particles can be embedded as deep as several feet, so it is often advisable to excavate this kind of bedrock material for its gold content.

Usuaully it is best to clean the bedrock as the rock progresses upstream. A final cleaning of the surface may be left until the end of the season when there is more time to spend on this activity and when the water is short for other work.

Where bedrock is hard it must be cleaned largely by hand, and the soft seams and cracks invariably present should be cleaned out with hand tools. A hose and small pump are almost necessities for a good cleanup. Sometimes a separate sluice box, smaller than that used in the main operation, will be pressed into service for handling materials from a cleanup operation.

Chapter Seven

SPECIAL CONDITIONS

DRY WASHERS HAVE been used for many years in the southwestern United States where water is scarce, particularly in New Mexico where some millions of dollars of gold have been produced during the past century by dry washing. The Cerillos, Hillsboro, and Golden districts are among those where considerable gold has been won without water. During the last big depression in the Thirties many men also used dry washers with success in Nevada, Arizona, and Southern California. A notable amount of gold has been accounted for in Australia, too, by such methods.

Placers where water action has been absent are different from those in the more usual places in that there is a lack of water-rounded pebbles. The gold itself, too, is frequently angular and rough, revealing for one thing a shorter distance of travel from its lode. Usually, the gold-bearing ground is bound together with lime or with iron oxide which must be broken up before the yellow scatterings can be recovered. Dry stream beds are likely places to look, while in more arid areas the metal is sometimes discovered where it has been washed downward and deposited by an infrequent cloudburst.

All in all, the richness per yard of a dry placer must be markedly greater than that in a creek bank or bar for three reasons; higher living costs, more expensive recovery procedures, and the fact that usually less of the gold is secured than would be the case with the usual sluiceway, although if conditions are right the reclamation of coarse gold can be remarkably thorough.

If the gravel is to be treated successfully by dry washing, it must be both completely dry and disintegrated. After a rainstorm, for example, operations must be curtailed until the ground dries out once more. Even in extremely dry climates, the gravel is slightly damp below the surface (the reason why solar stills are successful in the most arid of deserts) and must be dried out before it can be treated in a dry washer. Spreading the material to dry in the sun or putting it through driers adds still more to the cost of the mining. In small-scale work, however, it is true that the gravel will dry about as fast as it can be treated.

Dry washers are usually hand operations and have about the same capacity as regular rockers of corresponding size. The work of running the dry washer is much more difficult, however, The workers select the material they are to treat with regard to both dryness and likely gold content. It is difficult to do this on a large scale with hired labor.

Plants with mechanical excavators and complex power-driven dry-washing machinery have been tried, but in this country, at least, virtually all have been commercial failures, largely because the gravel was dug faster than the sun could dry it. Also in large-scale work, particularly with mechanical excavation, the cost of sizing the material can be exorbitant. Clay and cemented gravel introduce even further difficulties.

When the gold-bearing material is completely dry and disintegrated, panning tests of the tailings should show that a good saving can be made before any more work is attempted, except perhaps with extremely fine or flaky gold.

Completely disintegrated material is seldom obtained, however. The tops of clay streaks in the gravel are likely to be richer in gold than the gravel itself. Clay or cemented gravel seldom can be broken up sufficiently by hand to free all the gold without some sort of pulverizer. In a dry washer, unfortunately, all gold included in a lump of waste passes out of the machine. As water ordinarily will break up all the gravel and separate the gold, better savings usually can be effected with rocker or sluiceways than with a dry washer.

Basically, the dry washer separates gold from sand by pulsations of air through a porous medium. The screened gravel passes down an inclined riffle box with cross riffles. The bottom of the box consists of canvas or some other porous material. Under the riffle box is a bellows by which air is blown through the canvas in short, strong puffs. This gives a combination shaking and classifying motion to the material. The gold because of its weight gravitates to the canvas and is held by the riffles, while the waste passes out of the machine.

The gravel is first shoveled into a box, holding a few shovelfuls, at the head of the washer, from where it runs through the apparatus. A screen with about one-half-inch openings is used over the box, eliminating the larger stuff which, depending on the ground, may be watched for nuggets.

A DRY WASHER

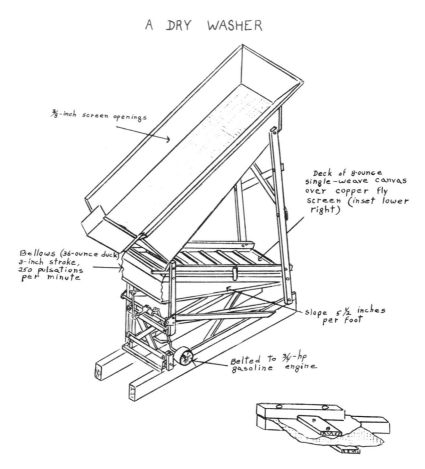

⅜-inch screen openings

Deck of 8-ounce single-weave canvas over copper fly screen (inset lower right)

Bellows (36-ounce duck) 3-inch stroke, 250 pulsations per minute

slope 5½ inches per foot

Belted to ¾-hp gasoline engine

May be powered by hand or machine

A dry washer is often run by a small gasoline engine, saving the labor of one man. The capacity of such a contrivance is considerably greater than that of one operated solely by hand. For instance, one man working alone without power must fill the box, then turn a crank which runs the bellows while all the gravel runs through. The process is then repeated. One man can treat from one-half to one cubic yard per day with a hand-operated washer. With two men working, one shovels and the other turns the crank.

When the time comes to clean up, the material behind the riffles is usually dumped into a pan and washed out in water. If water is extremely scarce, the accumulated substances from the riffles can be put through the machine a second time, then further cleaned by blowing away the lighter grains of sand from a pan.

Economically successful dry washers are usually handmade and have been built in a large number of sizes and designs. An example of one type is illustrated.

The bellows of this particular machine is made of 36-ounce duck and the bottom of the riffle box of 8-ounce single-weave canvas. In contrast to the single-weave canvas, silk or rayon permits a good extraction of gold, but too much dust goes through into the bellows. Heavier canvas is too tight for good separation. Copper-wire fly screen is used under the canvas.

The riffle box is 11 inches wide and 40 inches long. It contains six riffles. The slope of the riffle box is 5½ inches to the foot. Hand-operated machines are usually much smaller, and the riffle box is set at a steeper angle than with powered machines.

The gravel and sand are shoveled onto a screen with three-eights-inch openings at the top of the washer. The bellows is operated at 250 pulsations per minute, the stroke being three inches. The capacity of the machine is about four-fifths of a yard per hour which would probably correspond to from 1½ to two cubic yards bank measure. The plus one-inch material was previously discarded.

In cleaning up after treating approximately one cubic yard in the washer, the riffle box is lifted out and turned over on a large, flat surface such as a baking tin. The concentrate from the upper three riffles is first panned and the gold removed. Usually both the coarse and the fine gold can be saved here. The lower riffles may contain a few colors, but nearly all the gold is normally caught in the upper riffles.

SURF WASHER

Few sea-beach placer gold deposits have been mined successfully, the most important producers having been in the vicinity of Nome,

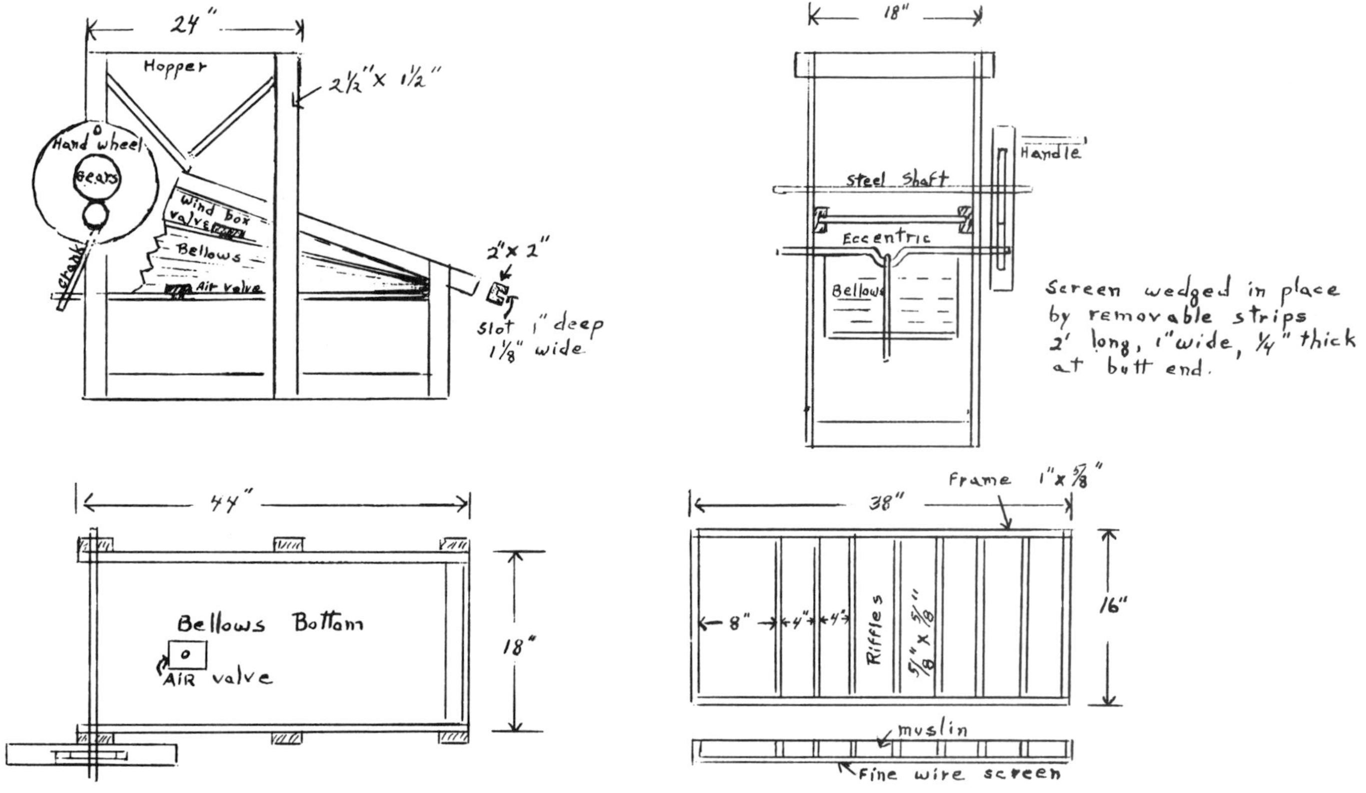

Screen wedged in place
by removable strips
2' long, 1" wide, ¼" thick
at butt end.

Handle

Steel Shaft

Eccentric

Bellows

18"

Frame 1" x ⅞"

16"

38"

Riffles

⅝" x ⅞"

8"

¼" x ¼" x ¼"

muslin

Fine wire screen

2" x 2"

slot ¼" deep
1⅛" wide

2½" x ½"

24"

Hopper

Hand wheel

Eccentric

Crank

Wind box
Valves

Bellows

Air valve

44"

18"

Bellows Bottom

Air valve

DRY WASHER

Alaska, But gold is also known to occur in a few other shorelines along states bordering the Pacific. Special techniques, therefore, have been developed to take advantage of the action of the surf in recovering the yellow metal from these deposits.

Surf washers are similar to Long Toms but are wider and shorter. They can be used, of course, only when the surf is at the proper height. They are set so an incoming wave rushes up the sluice, washes material from the screen box or hopper and, retracting, carries it over the riffles and plates. One man can often attend two surf washers, handling about eight cubic yards each 10 hours.

An example of a simple surf washer is a riffled sluice three to four feet wide and eight to 10 feet long, set on the sand at the water's edge so that the incoming waves wash through it to the upper end, then retract below the lower end. The sluice is made of boards that are nailed at either end to sills, which can be weighed down with rocks.

The sides are four or five inches high. The riffles in this particular instance are made of inch-square strips spaced about one inch apart. The end sections are transverse riffles, the center section longitudinal.

Preferably, the box is set on a grade of eight to 10 inches per 12 feet. Best results are obtained by using quicksilver in the riffles. When the surf is strong, the washer will treat as much as two men can shovel, but at other times it must be fed very slowly.

SKIN DIVING

Skin diving enthusiasts in recent years have taken up small-scale placer mining as a hobby and an occasionally profitable venture. Various kinds of apparel and equipment are used, but the investment is generally not great.

Wet suits and canvas shoes are almost necessities for entering cold mountain streams to search the beds for pockets that may contain gold. Beginners should be equipped with a snorkel, face mask, gloves, a weighted belt, fins, a crevicing tool, and a gold pan. More experienced divers may use the popular scuba equipment, but this calls for special knowledge to insure safety.

Crevicing tools include large spoons, tire irons, crowbars, and the like; almost anything that can reach into tight places and dislodge nuggets from the stream bottom. The pan should be used to test sands from various places where gold would be expected to settle, such as the downstream side of obstructions. Where colors in the pan indicate a favorable area of the stream, a more intensive search may be made.

SUCTION DREDGES

High-altitude suction dredging, or hydraulic sluicing, was pioneered by the Exanimo Establishment of Fremont, Nebraska 68025, which says any dredge that operates successfully at heights in excess of 9,000 feet will perform proportionally better at lower altitudes. One Spartan user, according to company president Paul F. Tainter, has reported 1,500 ounces recovered in Guatemala in one season, a second 6 ounces a week in Idaho with only spare-hour operation. Others tell of what they call exceptional recoveries in northern California and in bootleg placering operations in Oregon.

Tainter points to the unique riffle system incorporated in the Spartan flared sluice box, which combines coarse cocoa matting with an uncommon expanded metal. Most of the gold, he says, is retained before it ever gets to the first Hungarian riffle.

The second of the two most widely regarded manufacturers and suppliers "in 1960 built a 12-inch suction dredge, spent several summer months on the Trinity River in northern California, and dredged up 88 ounces of gold—mostly small nuggets," reminisces H. O. Fiedler. "We sold our gold during the early sixties for $42 an ounce, which at the $35 per ounce price at that time was good. Had we only kept our gold till now!"

Heading the Fiedler Equipment Co. at 10534 Brunswick Road in Grass Valley, California 95945, H. O. Fiedler has since been "hand-crafting" gold dredges and "catering to those who want old-fashioned workmanship." He describes the concern as "a small company with no desire to expand our manufacturing facilities even though we have been swamped with dredge orders for over a year." These include commissions for both shore-based and floating dredges, among them the portable 56-pound Surface Sluice Gold Dredge, as well as a similar but larger 66-pound model.

Chapter Eight

THE ODDS ARE LONG, BUT THE STAKES ARE HIGH

BECAUSE OF THE nature of gold—its heaviness, its resistance to tarnish and hence its high visibility, and its distinctive yellow color—the most useful tool in the search for deposits has been the gold pan, with which gold can be recognized immediately if it is in large enough particles.

The gold pan is still a most useful instrument, but it is unreliable for detecting either gold terrurides or extremely fine grained gold such as that characterizing the Carlin-type deposits, now believed by many to hold a primary hope for today's prospector. For measurement of unseen gold in rock samples, the fire assay has until recently been the standard method.

However, the fire assay is both costly and time-consuming and has been supplanted to a large degree by atomic absorption spectrophotometry, an economical and swift method that can detect as little as 20 parts per billion in a sample. This system has made possible the routine analysis of large numbers of samples, thus greatly facilitating the exploration for gold.

EXPLORING THE DISCOVERY

Your initial concern after locating a gold prospect and deciding it is worth working will be to determine its width and length. It will be equally important to know whether or not it runs continuously between natural exposures.

The general sequence of exploration methods includes panning, stripping, trenching, test-pitting, shallow diamond drilling, sampling, and mapping. These steps must be adapted to local conditions and to other factors during the exploration campaign such as: progress of work, results obtained, finances, availability of supplies, labor, etc.

Panning

Panning will usually reveal if a vein, shear area, or mineralized region carries any gold where it is exposed and, if so, whether the gold is present in sufficient amounts and with enough regularity to warrant further work.

If the width and lateral extent of the deposit are not already sufficiently exposed, a limited amount of work will usually be done by the prospector. In the simplest of instances it may only involve the scraping off of moss or thin overburden. If necessary, this will be supplemented by digging trenches.

If the deposit is revealed in an outcrop or trench, it will generally be useful to drive in a stake or to place a pile of rocks to mark its center if it is narrow or to designate its walls, and to set other such markers along the strike to assist in positioning trenches.

If the deposit seems to end in one direction, it will be good practice to do some further stripping or trenching in the vicinity in an effort to learn if it actually dies out, if it is faulted, or if branches or parallel bodies can be located.

Next, it may be necessary to consider whether to blast into the rock. Many deposits are too weathered to allow proper examination unless fresh openings are made as by blasting.

Stripping

Assuming that panning of exposed portions of the vein or zone has been encouraging, the next step will be to strip moss and overburden concealing sections between exposures or to find possible extensions. The purpose will be to obtain a rough estimate of the length and width of the vein.

Where overburden is less than a foot or two deep and the vein is less than a foot wide, stripping may be done along the vein strike. Otherwise, it is better to put in trenches at regular intervals of from 10 to 100 feet, depending on:

(a) Width of vein and shearing.
(b) Regularity of vein structure.
(c) Depth of overburden, accessibility.

Generally, the work can be done without explosives unless the soil is frozen or unless the overburden forms part of a clayey or boulder-filled muskeg. Tools required include pick, shovel, mattock, and sounding bar or bull point. The work can be done by one or two men.

Trenching

The purpose of trenching is to expose a portion of fresh unoxidized vein or shear material to ensure proper sampling. The work is often done concurrently with stripping on a showing. No stripping will be required, however, where the vein is not covered by overburden.

If the rock is solid and unweathered, there will be no advantage in going down more than one foot at maximum. If values increase with depth as is popularly supposed by some, it will be with depths of twenties to hundreds of feet, not with additional single feet. Any trenches should be numbered and a picket line or marked stakes used for mapping purposes.

SAMPLING

A good sample is the cutting of a representative part of a vein or shear that as nearly as possible represents its average value. Judgment and a certain amount of practical experience are essential for an honest sample.

The purpose of this work is to determine as accurately as possible the dollar value per ton of rock in the vein or waste. Trenching, diamond drilling, and underground work are sometimes undertaken to enable proper sampling, as well as to obtain geological and other information about the prospect.

Mineral deposits are generally much smaller in one dimension than in the others, and this smaller dimension is the width. For this reason, samples should be cut across the deposit and not along it. The most acceptable section for sampling is at right angles to the walls of the deposit. The important dimension of any sample is the width which it represents.

A sample should contain all the minerals in the same proportion as they exist in the material sampled, as well as holding the same volume of material from each inch of width sampled.

The precious metals such as gold are usually very irregularly distributed through the rock in which they exist, perhaps quartz. If the rock being sampled is composed of both hard and soft materials, there will be a natural tendency to include more of the softer substance. When this is a schist, the softer material is sometimes the richer. To be truly representative, however, the sample must contain the proper proportion of all its parts regardless of the ease or difficulty in breaking it out.

From one to two pounds of material is usually taken per foot of width. In other words, the sample from a vein three feet wide should weigh about three to 4½ pounds. Where there are marked differences of hardness or of mineralization, more dependable results will be secured if the total width to be sampled is divided into parts, each of which consists of material of about the same hardness and degree of mineralization, a separate sample being taken from each part.

In any event, the maximum width from which a single sample is taken is ordinarily not more than three to five feet. If a lode is wider than five feet, two or more samples should be taken.

Of the various methods of sampling, three in common use by prospectors follow:

1. Grab Samples

This is a pick of better than average pieces of mineralized vein material for sampling, being therefore not truly representative. Upon discovery of gold and as a preliminary step in examining its occurrence, this type of sample is frequently taken so as to indicate the distribution of values and the kind of mineralization with which the values are associated.

2. Chip Samples

These are similar to channel samples, except that instead of cutting a channel, pieces or chips are knocked off at intervals of every one or few inches across a vein or occurrence. This is often done with a prospector's hammer.

During the course of taking this kind of sample, should a larger than average piece be split off it should be broken to the average size. Care should be exercised in taking chip samples for assay, as these will determine the estimate of the average value of a particular section. While results of this type of sampling are not as accurate as channel sampling, they should if well taken check fairly close with the results from channel samples.

3. Channel Samples

The first requisite is that the surface to be sampled be thoroughly cleaned with a broom or wire brush. The strip to be channeled, two to three inches wide, should be marked off by chalk or crayon. Then with hammer or other tool remove all material within the strip lines to a uniform depth of one-half to one inch deep across the width of the vein.

Care must be taken to obtain any finely broken material, as some of the metalliferous minerals are shattered to dust during the cutting of a channel. This material cut from the channel can be caught on a sampling sheet of canvas, in a box, gold pan, or large can. A pound or more is generally secured from each linear foot of channel.

If there are any variations in mineralization and character within the vein, these should be sampled separately wherever practical. Separate samples should also be taken of the wall rock at each side of the deposit in the event that it contains valuable minerals. Where the deposit is uniform, a length of not more than four feet of channel should be regarded as one sample, separate samples being taken if a deposit is more than four feet wide. Instances or length of channel, mentioned as width in your records, should be given in tenths of a foot rather than inches for ease of calculation.

All pertinent information relative to the sample should be entered in the sample book; date, property name, vein and trench number, width of sample, description of vein, for what metals to be assayed, and the initials or name of the sampler. For a more permanent record, it is best to mark the number of the sample either by painting on the rock or by marking with crayon or soft lead pencil on a short stake which is then precisely placed within the trench.

Most sample books have detachable portions on each sheet, with a corresponding number on the part retained in the book. The detachable portion of the sample book, after being properly marked, is folded and placed in the filled sample bag which is then tied at the neck and set aside in the trench. This procedure is than repeated with the next sample either in the same trench or the next one.

Precautions should be taken: (a) to avoid mixing samples by not following the above routine and especially by putting sample tags on the wrong bags; (b) to avoid accidental salting of samples by not using clean bags, by not cleaning the sampling canvas after each use, or by not cleaning off the trench rocks to be sampled.

FREE MINERAL IDENTIFICATION

Although the Bureau of Mines, U.S. Department of the Interior, Washington, D.C. 20240 does not provide analytical services to the general public, it does maintain a free mineral identification service. For this purpose, specimens may be sent to any of the below U.S. Bureau of Mines laboratories. Each should be securely packaged and have a firmly attached label indicating where the particular sample was secured and furnishing the sender's name and address. A letter giving the particulars should be included.

Reno Metallurgy Research Center
1605 Evans Avenue
Reno, Nevada 89505

Salt Lake City Metallurgy Research Center
1600 East First South
Salt Lake City, Utah 84112

Tuscaloosa Metallurgy Research Center
P.O. Box L
University, Alabama 35486

Albany Metallurgy Research Center
Box 70
Albany, Oregon 97231

Boulder City Metallurgy Research Laboratory
500 Dale Street
Boulder City, Nevada 89005

College Park Metallurgy Research Center
College Park, Maryland 20740

Twin Cities Metallurgy Research Center
P.O. Box 1660
Twin City Airport, Minnesota 55111

Rolla Metallurgy Research Center
P.O. Box 280
Rolla, Missouri 55401

OTHER FACILITIES

The experimental plant of the Colorado School of Mines, Golden, Colorado 80401 will identify mineral samples free if they come from Colorado and if the exact location from which the sample was taken is given.

Although there are no facilities in the area for free chemical analyses or assays, a free mineral identification service limited to samples from New Mexico is maintained at the New Mexico State Bureau of Mines and Mineral Resources, Socorro, New Mexico 87801.

A laboratory is maintained at College, Alaska 99701 by the Department of Natural Resources, Division of Geological Survey, to provide free analytical work on Alaskan samples for Alaskan prospectors. Services include fire assays for gold and silver, atomic absorption analyses, spectrographic analyses, analyses by X-ray flourescence and X-ray diffraction, and mineralogic examinations. Samples may be mailed or delivered directly to the lab. A sample assay request supplied by the Division must be filled out and submitted with each sample.

Incidentally, the Division of Geological Survey staff includes a mining engineer who is available for the free examination of Alaskan properties for prospectors who are unable to afford the services of a private engineer. This help includes advice on how to proceed with the prospect, its probable worth at the time examined, and if desired a written report on the prospect. Requests for this type of assistance should be accompanied by information on the location, nature, and extent of the deposit, together with samples and assay reports. The Division's services even include making contacts with prospective purchasers when requested.

Idaho's Bureau of Mines and Geology, Moscow, Idaho 83843 maintains a qualitative mineral identification service for samples originating in Idaho or from Idaho citizens. No assaying or quantitative chemical analysis is provided.

The Mineral Development Division, Department of Mines and Energy, St. John's, Newfoundland provides a free mineral identification service. Samples may be assayed by the Division's laboratory if such assays are warranted in the opinion of the Division's staff.

The Arizona Bureau of Mines offers a free mineral identification to residents of Arizona who submit materials from that State. A charge of two dollars per specimen is made for samples submitted from outside the State. Samples should be sent to the Arizona Bureau of Mines, University of Arizona, Tuscon, Arizona 85721. The Bureau, however, does not engage in making quantitative assays to determine the potential value of samples.

The Geological Survey of Canada, Department of Energy, Mines and Resources, 601 Booth, Ottawa, Ontario offers an identification of rocks and does not include analysis or assay.

The Montana Bureau of Mines and Geology, Butte, Montana 59701 provides a free mineral-identification service for residents of Montana and for residents of other areas if their samples were collected in Montana. This service does not include quantitative analysis or assaying. However, you will get mineral or rock identification, a statement of possible economic value and of possible markets if marketable, and suggestions for further action if warranted. Specimens submitted to the Mineral Identification Laboratory should be about one by two by three inches and in their natural state; not sawed, polished, crushed, or melted. Placer sand or gravel should be panned to a heavy concentrate.

Free assays in the Yukon Territory are available only to accredited Canadian prospectors who are receiving grants under the Prospectors' Assistance Act, according to the Office of the Resident Geologist, Indian and Northern Affairs, Room 211, Federal Building, Whitehorse, Yukon Territory.

A prospector who has claims registered in Quebec can get "for the asking" coupons exchangeable for a certain number of assays; that is, five coupons per mining certificate, good for five gold assays. The certificate, at a cost of 10 dollars, allows a prospector to stake 200 acres of mining land, according to the Resident Geologist, Department of Natural Resources, 158 Bourlamaque Boulevard, Val d'Or, P. Q.

When mining claims are recorded in Manitoba, it is the practice of the Department of Mines, Resources, and Environmental Management, Mine Branch, 904 Norquay Building, Winnipeg, Manitoba to issue two free assay coupons. The samples are assayed by the Department's laboratory.

"If you merely want identification as to what can be seen by the naked eye, most Departments of Geology or State Geological Surveys would be able to help you with the identification," according to State Geologist Duncan J. McGregor, South Dakota Geological Survey, Science Center, University, Vermillion, South Dakota 57069. "There are no firms in the State of South Dakota that analyze rocks free of charge."

The Analytical Branch of the British Columbia Department of Mines and Petroleum Resources, Victoria, B.C. will perform free assays on five samples submitted between May 1 and September by a bona fide prospector in possession of a valid British Columbia Free Miner's License. These licenses are now issued only to Canadian citizens.

Ontario's Ministry of Natural Resources offers a service to prospectors through the Mineral Research Branch, located at 77 Granville Street, Toronto, Ontario. The branch laboratory will give free evaluation of samples that are sent in by Ontario prospectors, and a complete analysis is available and may be paid for with coupons issued with the recording of mining claims.

On the other hand, the Department of Mineral Resources, Regina, Saskatchewan does not have any service for free assays of samples for the general public, although there is a provincial School for Prospectors at LaRonge, Saskatchewan, that can help with general identification.

"Many mining companies will analyze ores, including gold, for established prospectors," according to the Mineral Resources Branch, Department of Natural Resources, P.O. Box 1260, Fredericton, New Brunswick. There are no laboratories otherwise in the Province that carry out free gold assays.

The State Department of Geology and Mineral Industries, 1069 State Office Building, Portland, Oregon 97201 will assay for gold at three dollars per sample or for gold and silver at four dollars per sample. There is no limit to the number of samples, and they need not be from Oregon.

STATE GEOLOGISTS

Pertinent, up-to-date, local information may also be secured from the following list of State Geologists. States not included in this roster have no geologist nor State Mineral Agency.

State	Name and Title	Address & Telephone Number
Alabama	Mr. Philip E. LaMoreaux, State Geologist	Geological Survey of Alabama P.O. Drawer O University, Alabama 35486 205-759-5721
Alaska	Mr. William C. Fackler, Asst. Commissioner	Department of Natural Resources 3001 Porcupine Drive Anchorage, Alaska 99504 907-279-1433

State	*Name and Title*	*Address & Telephone Number*
Arizona	Dr. William H. Dresher, Director	Arizona Bureau of Mines University of Arizona Tucson, Arizona 85721 602-884-2733
Arkansas	Mr. Norman F. Williams, State Geologist	Arkansas Geological Commission State Capitol Bldg. Little Rock, Arkansas 72201 501-371-1646
California	Mr. Wesley G. Bruer, State Geologist and Chief	Division of Mines and Geology California Department of Conservation Resources Bldg. P.O. Box 2980 Sacramento, Calif. 95814 916-445-1825
Colorado	Mr. John W. Rold, Director and State Geologist	Colorado Geological Survey 254 Columbine Bldg. 1845 Sherman Street Denver, Colorado 80203 303-892-2611
Connecticut	Dr. Joe Webb Peoples, Director	Connecticut Geological and Natural History Survey Box 128, Wesleyan Station Middletown, Connecticut 06457 203-346-0788
Delaware	Dr. Robert R. Jordan, State Geologist	Delaware Geological Survey University of Delaware 16 Robinson Hall Newark, Delaware 19711 302-738-2568
Florida	Dr. Charles Hendry, Jr., State Geologist and Division Director	Department of National Resources Bureau of Geology P.O. Box 631 Tallahassee, Florida 32302 904-224-7141
Georgia	Mr. Sam M. Pickering, Jr., State Geologist and Director	Earth & Water Division Department of Natural Resources 19 Hunter Street, S.W. Atlanta, Georgia 30334 404-656-3214

State	Name and Title	Address & Telephone Number
Hawaii	Mr. Robert T. Chuck, Manager-Chief Engineer	Division of Water & Land Development Department of Land & Natural Resources P.O. Box 373 Honolulu, Hawaii 96809 808-548-2211
Idaho	Dr. Rolland R. Reid, Director	Idaho Bureau of Mines & Geology Moscow, Idaho 83843 208-885-6111
Illinois	Dr. John C. Frye, Chief	Illinois State Geological Survey 121 Natural Resources Bldg. Urbana, Illinois 61801 217-344-1481
Indiana	Dr. John B. Patton, State Geologist	Department of Natural Resources Geological Survey 611 N. Walnut Grove Bloomington, Indiana 47401 812-337-5582
Iowa	Dr. Samuel J. Tuthill, Director and State Geologist	Iowa Geological Survey Geological Survey Bldg. 16 West Jefferson Street Iowa City, Iowa 52240 319-338-1173
Kansas	Dr. William W. Hambleton, State Geologist and Director	State Geological Survey of Kansas The University of Kansas Lawrence, Kansas 66044 913-864-3101
Kentucky	Dr. Wallace W. Hagan, Director and State Geologist	Kentucky Geological Survey University of Kentucky 307 Mineral Industries Bldg. Lexington, Kentucky 40506 606-258-8991
Louisiana	Mr. Leo W. Hough, State Geologist	Louisiana Geological Survey Box G. University Station Baton Rouge, Louisiana 70803 504-348-2201

State	Name and Title	Address & Telephone Number
Maine	Dr. Robert G. Doyle, State Geologist	Main Geological Survey State Office Bldg., Rm. 211 Augusta, Maine 04330 207-289-2801
Maryland	Dr. Kenneth N. Weaver, Director	Maryland Geological Survey 214 Latrobe Hall, John Hopkins University Baltimore, Maryland 21218 301-235-0771
Massachusetts	Mr. Joseph A. Sinnott, State Geologist	Massachusetts Dept. of Public Works Research & Material Div. 99 Worcester Street Wellesley, Massachusetts 12181 617-237-9110
Michigan	Mr. Arthur E. Slaughter, State Geologist	Department of Natural Resources Geological Survey Division Stevens T. Mason Bldg. Lansing, Michigan 48926 517-373-1256
Minnesota	Dr. Paul K. Sims, Director	Minnesota Geological Survey University of Minnesota 1633 Eustis Street St. Paul, Minnesota 55108 612-373-3590
Mississippi	Mr. William H. Moore, Director and State Geologist	Mississippi Geological, Economic & Topographical Survey Drawer 4915 Jackson, Mississippi 39216 601-362-1056
Missouri	Dr. Wallace B. Howe, State Geologist and Director	Division of Geological Survey & Water Resources P.O. Box 250 Rolla, Missouri 65401 314-364-1752
Montana	Dr. S. L. Groff Acting Director and State Geologist	Montana Bureau of Mines & Geology Montana College of Mineral Science and Technology Butte, Montana 59701 406-792-8321

State	Name and Title	Address & Telephone Number
Nebraska	Mr. Vincent H. Dreeszen, Director and State Geologist	Conservation & Survey Division University of Nebraska 113 Nebraska Hall Lincoln, Nebraska 68508 402-472-3471
Nevada	Dr. Vernon E. Scheid, Director	Nevada Bureau of Mines University of Nevada Reno, Nevada 89507 702-784-6987
New Hampshire	Dr. Glenn W. Stewart, State Geologist	Department of Resources & Economic Development Geologic Branch, Dept. of Geology James Hall, University of New Hampshire Durham, New Hampshire 03824 603-862-1216
New Jersey	Dr. Kemble Widmer, State Geologist	New Jersey Bureau of Geology & Topography John Fitch Plaza, Rm. 709 P.O. Box 1889 Trenton, New Jersey 08625 609-292-2576
New Mexico	Mr. Don H. Baker, Jr., Director	New Mexico State Bureau of Mines & Mineral Resources Campus Station Socorro, New Mexico 87801 505-835-5420
New York	Dr. James F. Davis, State Geologist	New York State Museum & Science Service Geological Survey New York State Education Building, Rm. 973 Albany, New York 12224 518-474-5816
North Carolina	Mr. Stephen G. Conrad, State Geologist	Division of Mineral Resources Department of Natural & Economic Resources P.O. Box 27687 Raleigh, North Carolina 27611

State	Name & Title	Address & Telephone Number
North Dakota	Dr. Edwin A. Noble, State Geologist	North Dakota Geological Survey University Station Grand Forks, North Dakota 58202 701-777-2231
Ohio	Mr. Horace R. Collins, Division Chief and State Geologist	Ohio Division of Geological Survey 1207 Grandview Avenue Columbus, Ohio 43212 614-469-5344
Oklahoma	Dr. Charles J. Mankin, Director	Oklahoma Geological Survey The University of Oklahoma Norman, Oklahoma 73069 405-325-3031
Oregon	Mr. Raymond E. Corcoran, State Geologist	State Dept. of Geology & Mineral Industries 1069 State Office Bldg. 1400 S.W. Fifth Avenue Portland, Oregon 97201 503-229-5580
Pennsylvania	Dr. Arthur A. Socolow, Director	Bureau of Topographic & Geological Survey Dept. of Environmental Resources Harrisburg, Pennsylvania 17120 717-787-2169
South Carolina	Mr. Norman E. Olson, State Geologist	Division of Geology P.O. Box 927 Columbia, South Carolina 29202 803-758-3257
South Dakota	Dr. Duncan J. McGregor, State Geologist	South Dakota State Geological Survey Science Center, University of South Dakota Vermillion, South Dakota 57069 605-624-4471
Tennessee	Mr. Robert E. Hershey, State Geologist	Department of Conservation Division of Geology G-5 State Office Bldg. Nashville, Tennessee 37219 615-741-2726

State	Name & Title	Address & Telephone Number
Texas	Dr. W. L. Fisher, Director	Bureau of Economic Geology University of Texas at Austin Austin, Texas 78712 512-471-1534
Utah	Dr. William F. Hewitt, Director	Utah Geological & Mineralogical Survey 103 Utah Geological Survey Bldg. University of Utah Salt Lake City, Utah 84112 801-322-6831
Vermont	Dr. Charles G. Doll, State Geologist	Vermont Geological Survey University of Vermont Burlington, Vermont 05401 802-864-4511
Virginia	Dr. James L. Calver, State Geologist and Commissioner	Virginia Division of Mineral Resources P.O. Box 3667 Charlottesville, Virginia 22903 703-293-5121
Washington	Mr. Vaughn E. Livingston, Acting Supervisor	Washington Division of Mines & Geology Department of Natural Resources P.O. Box 168 Olympia, Washington 98501 206-753-6183

COMMERCIAL ASSAYERS

You may find a nearby commercial assayer in the yellow pages of your telephone directory. If not, there follows a list of some of the commercial laboratories that perform gold and silver assays. Any of these concerns should be queried in advance as to fees, size and type of samples desired, and other pertinent information.

Ledoux and Company
359 Alfred Avenue
Teaneck, New Jersey 07666

Colorado Assaying Company
2013 Welton Street
Denver, Colorado 80205

Metallurgical Laboratories, Inc.
1142 Howard Street
San Francisco, California 94103

California Testing Labs
619 E. Washington Boulevard
Los Angeles, California 90015

Southwestern Assayers & Chemists
710 East Evans Boulevard
Tucson, Arizona 85713

Canadian Testing Association
696 Yonge Street
Toronto, Ontario

J. T. Donald & Co., Ltd.
1181 Guy Street
Montreal, Quebec

Technical Service Laboratories
325 Howe Street
Vancouver, British Columbia

Chapter Nine

GETTING PAID TO PROSPECT

THE U. S. GOVERNMENT will even pay you to prospect for gold. The U.S. Geological Survey, through its Office of Minerals Exploration, encourages exploration for gold and certain other minerals within the United States, its Territories, and its Possessions. The program provides financial assistance on a participating basis.

This assistance is available to those who would not ordinarily undertake the proposed exploration at their sole expense and who are unable to obtain the necessary finances from commercial sources at reasonable terms.

Exploration may be conducted from the surface or underground, using recognized and sound procedures, including standard geophysical and geochemical methods, to obtain geological and mineralogical information in favorable areas.

An applicant for assistance must own, lease, or have an otherwise valid claim to the property he wishes to explore. The U. S. does not grubstake nor finance prospecting expeditions. A reasonable probability must exist for significant discovery of ore on the property, and the property and workings must be accessible for examination. The applicant must also show that he has adequate means to start the proposed work and continue it until the Governmental funds begin to arrive. Repayment to the Government is at the rate of five percent royalty on actual production from the property. There is no requirement for you to produce, and if there is no production, no repayment is required.

Answers to the questions most frequently asked by applicants follow. For further information, write to the office listed on the last page of this chapter.

How may you become eligible for exploration assistance?

To be eligible for gold exploration assistance by the Government, you must:

1. Have a sufficient interest in property which can qualify for gold exploration,

2. Furnish evidence that funds for the exploration are not available from banking institutions or from other commercial sources of credit on reasonable terms,

3. Certify that you would not ordinarily undertake the proposed exploration under current conditions and circumstances at your sole expense.

What is meant by a "sufficient interest?"

A "sufficient interest" gives you the right of possession of a property both for the length of time required to complete the exploration and to protect the Government's interest thereafter. Obviously, unencumbered ownership is sufficient. A located claim or a leasehold, preferably with renewal rights, may also be enough.

If you are leasing the property, what must you obtain from your landlord?

You should obtain a lien agreement from your landlord, using Lien and Subordination Agreements (MME Form 52) supplied by the Office of Minerals Exploration. If the agreement may not be obtained, you should provide the Office of Minerals Exploration with a copy of the letter of refusal. The Office may then accept, in lieu of the agreement, a performance bond (using 5, Standard Form 25 supplied by the Office) executed by an approved corporate surety or two responsible individual sureties.

If the property is subject to a mortgage, lien, or other encumbrance, what document should you provide to the Government?

You must obtain a subordination agreement from the mortgagee, using MME Form 52, or provide a performance bond before an exploration contract may be executed.

Why must you deal with your landlord if you are leasing or with your mortgagee if your interest is subject to a mortgage?

The lien or subordination agreement, or the performance bond in lieu thereof, is required to secure the payment of royalty to the Government on any production during the exploration work or after certification if a certificate of possible production is issued.

Would you be eligible under this program if you have no interest in a property and wish to purchase or lease the property only if you may get aid from the Government?

No, but you could become eligible by entering into an agreement to purchase or lease the property subject to obtaining an exploration contract.

What evidence must you give that funds are not available on reasonable terms from commercial sources?

You must furnish evidence of your efforts to obtain credit from two banking institutions or other commercial sources of credit. This evidence must include true copies of your letters showing the amount and terms requested and proposed use of loan funds, as well as true copies of the replies showing why such a loan was not granted.

Will other evidence of financial eligibiliby be required?

You must give assurance that your share of the exploration costs can be furnished. You may also be required to furnish additional information including a financial statement.

Must you be an experienced operator or miner?

Not necessarily, but you will be reponsible for securing competent and experienced people to supervise the exploration if an exploration contract is executed.

How may you obtain financial assistance for gold exploration?

You should file an application for assistance on MME Form 40 in duplicate, triplicate for Alaska, answering all the questions to the best of your ability. Application forms may be secured by writing to the Office of Minerals Exploration, U.S. Geological Survey, Washington, D.C. 20242 or to the nearest field office, the address of which is given at the end of this chapter.

What information is required in your application?

Your application must include the following information:

1. Evidence that funds are not available to you upon reasonable terms from commercial sources;

2. A legal description of the property to be explored;

3. A statement of your interest in the property;

4. A description of the pertinent geology of the property;

5. An explanation of your reasons for expecting to find gold in profitable amounts;

6. An explicit statement of the proposed exploration work;

7. A listing of the cost estimates for the labor, materials, and equipment that will be required for the project;

8. A detailed estimate of the cost of each type of work separately;

9. Maps showing land boundaries, existing workings, and proposed work.

How may you obtain help in gathering the information and preparing the application?

You may consult with the Officer of Minerals Exploration, or with the Washington office, on any question that arises. If you are not experienced in mining or exploration, you may need a consulting mining engineer or geologist to help you with some of the information. The application form contains full instructions. The general instructions on the front of the form tell you what to do, and each item of information is described in detail on the back.

May the work include blocking out ore for production?

No. The regulations state, "The work shall not go beyond a reasonable delineation and sampling of a mineral deposit, and shall not be conducted primarily for mining or preparation for mining."

What action does the Office of Minerals Exploration take upon your application?

The application is reviewed to determine if the information requested has been submitted. If not, the applicant may be asked to furnish the missing information. When the application is complete, and if the facts warrant, a field examination of the property may be made by the Government, usually with the applicant, before a final decision is reached. A Governmental field examination is not made merely at the request of the applicant.

How does the Office of Minerals Exploration decide whether or not to approve an application?

The following factors will be considered in passing upon applications:

1. The geological probability of making a significant gold discovery,

2. The estimated cost of the exploration work in relation to the probable size and grade of the potential deposit,

3. The plan and method of conducting the exploration work,

4. The accessibility of the project area,

5. Your background and operating experience,

6. Your title or right to possession of the property.

If an application is approved, what further action is taken?

The Office of Minerals Exploration offers you an exploration contract.

What is the nature of an exploration contract?

The contract is an agreement between the Government and the operator. The details of the contract may vary to suit the individual project. However, the essential obligations in each contract are that the Government will contribute to the costs of the exploration work and that the operator will perform the work and repay the Government's contribution with interest by royalty on any production from the property.

What are the principal elements of an exploration contract?

The contract includes the following:

1. A description of the land upon which the work will be performed,

2. A detailed statement of the work to be done,

3. A time limit, generally not more than two years, within which the work must be completed.

4. An estimate of costs,

5. Provisions for the Government's contribution (not more than

the percent specified or $250,000) to costs and to repayment with interest to the Government in the event of production.

The contract also includes the standard provisions relating to non-discrimination, settlement of disputes, the eight-hour law, and rebate of wages.

Is more than one form of contract used?

Yes, two contract forms are presently used. Under the short form (MME Form 51) the Government's contribution is a percentage of unit costs of the work, agreed upon in advance and fixed by the contract. Under the long form (MME Form 50) the Government's contribution is a percentage of the allowable actual costs of the work as incurred or a combination of actual and fixed unit costs.

What are fixed unit costs?

The "fixed unit costs" of the work (per foot of drilling, per foot of drifting, per cubic yard of materials moved, etc.) are those agreed upon and set forth in the contract. The Government's contribution is a percentage of these fixed unit costs of work performed, verified by the representatives of the Office of Minerals Exploration as having been completed and found acceptable under the specifications of the Office's contract.

If a fixed unit cost in the contract is lower than the actual cost of the work, on which amount will the Government's contribution be based?

The contract holds. In other words, the Government's contribution will be based on the amount stated in the contract, whether the actual cost is greater or less. For example, if the fixed unit cost of drifting is $30 a foot and the actual cost is $35 a foot, the Government's contribution will be based on $30. And vice versa.

Are you required to complete all units of work specified in a fixed unit cost contract regardless of the actual costs per unit?

Yes, because this is what you agreed to do under that form of contract. However, under certain circumstances the number of units may be reduced by mutual agreement.

What is meant by "allowable costs" in the actual cost contract?

"Allowable costs" to which the Government will contribute are the direct costs of the work specified by the contract, such as labor, supervision, materials, supplies, and equipment. These costs must be supported by documentary evidence available for audit. Indirect costs, such as general overhead and corporate management expense, are not so-called allowable costs.

Is the cost of the work performed before the date of the contract with the Government allowable?

No.

If the work provided for in an actual cost contract cannot be completed within the estimated total cost, what are your obligations?

Your obligations under the contract vary to suit the circumstances of your project. Uusually your share of the estimated total allowable cost stated in the contract will be the limit of your obligation. However, the contract may require you to complete certain items of work at your own expense above the maximums fixed for those items by the contract.

Who determines whether a fixed unit cost or actual cost contract is to be used, and what factors are taken into consideration?

The Government decides which would be more appropriate in each individual case, depending on the estimated costs, the size and type of operation, etc. A unit cost contract is a much simpler document than an actual cost contract. It is easier to administer and is generally preferable, both to you and the Government, when the unit costs may be reasonably estimated in advance.

In what other way is a fixed unit cost contract simpler than an actual cost contract?

Under the fixed unit cost contract, the operator is not required by the Government to maintain itemized cost records or to submit documentary invoices of the actual costs incurred. There's a lot less paper work.

May rehabilitation of old workings be allowed as a part of the cost of exploration?

Yes, in certain cases limited rehabilitation may be provided by the contract when considered necessary to conduct the exploration work.

May permanent installations and improvements, or their rehabilitation, be allowed as part of the cost of the exploration work?

Yes, but only to the extent necessary to conduct the exploration work provided in the contract.

May the cost of operating equipment be included?

Yes, in one of the three following ways.

1. Depreciation is allowed on equipment owned by the operator to the extent of 1/60th of its fair market value or of its book value, whichever is less, for each month it is used on the project.

2. Rental of equipment not owned by the operator is allowed at reasonable rates.

3. Purchase of equipment is allowed, in which case the Government has an equity in the salvage value.

What becomes of equipment purchased or installations made to which the Government has contributed?

The Government owns them jointly with the operator in proportion to the amounts contributed, although title will be in the name of the operator. The Government's interest in any salable or salvageable property must be liquidated and accounted for when the Government's obligation to contribute to costs terminates or when the property is no longer needed for the work.

May you retain such equipment and installations for your own use?

Yes, but at a price at least as high as that which could be obtained by its sale to others.

Will you be given any allowance for the use or acquisition of the land and any existing buildings or installations thereon?

No, they and all fixtures are devoted to the project without allowance.

Will the cost of necessary rehabilitation or repair of existing buildings or installations be allowed?

Yes, the contract may allow these costs for work performed after the contract has been executed if such rehabilitation or repair is necessary for the exploratory work.

If the operator is an individual, a partnership, or a corporation, may the services of the individual, the partners, or a corporate officer be charged as allowable costs of the work?

The answer to this question is, importantly, yes, to the extent that the time and services of each are devoted exclusively and directly to the performance of the work, that they are qualified to perform the services, and that the services are provided for in the contract.

Who is to perform the exploration work?

You or your employees may handle the work, or the exploration contract may provide for an independent contractor to take care of all or any part of the work.

Will the Government give you any technical aid in the conduct of the exploration?

Yes, representatives of the Government will inspect the project from time to time and will be available for advice. However, the Government assumes no responsibility for the performance of the work, and unless you are qualified to direct the work yourself, you will be required to employ competent technical help.

If it is found after some of the work described in the contract has been done that it should proceed in another direction or be replaced by another type of work, may these changes be authorized?

Yes, inasmuch as both you and the Government benefit when the work proceeds in the most effective manner possible, the contract may be amended accordingly.

Suppose it is found while the work is in progress or upon its completion that additional work is needed to accomplish the original purpose of the contract? Then may such additional work be authorized?

Yes, in a suitable case the contract may be amended to provide for additional work and for a related increase in the estimate of the total allowable cost. However, the Government's contribution may not exceed a quarter of a million dollars.

If after some of the work has been done it becomes evident to you that there would be no advantage in completing the job, may the contract be terminated short of completion?

Yes, if the Government agrees with you, it will terminate the work by mutual agreement. If it does not agree, you may be required to complete the job. Should you discontinue the project or abandon it altogether without the Government's agreement, you would obviously be subject to a claim for damages or other remedy the law might provide for breach of contract.

Who is responsible for any damages to persons or property arising out of negligence in the course of the work?

You are, the work being entirely under your direction and control.

What reports will you have to make as the work progresses?

You have to submit a two-part monthly report to the Government. The first part of this is a monthly voucher claiming costs for contribution by the Government. In the instance of actual cost contracts, costs must be supported by certified true copies of invoices, transcripts of payrolls, etc. The second part is a concise narrative description of the work performed, results obtained, and any unusual situations encountered. It may be illustrated and supported by engineering-geological maps or sketches, drill hole logs, assay reports, etc. The voucher form (Form 9-1648) is furnished by the Government.

Is any final report necessary?

Yes, upon the completion or termination of the work, you must furnish the Government with an acceptable final report, giving a summary of the work performed under the contract and costs thereof, together with pertinent geologic and engineering data and an estimate of any ore reserves resulting from the exploration work.

What records will you have to keep?

For either a fixed unit cost contract or an actual cost contract you should maintain records, in accordance with the items to be reported on a voucher for reimbursement. For a fixed unit cost contract itemized cost records are not required by the Government. For an actual cost contract a simple distribution sheet is usually sufficient for small projects. Large projects, however, require more formal cost accounts. For either a small or large project under an actual cost contract, documentary support in the form of invoices, payrolls, tax returns, etc. must be available for audit.

May the Government inspect and audit your records and accounts?

Yes, either by its own auditors or by a certified public accountant. In virtually all cases, an appointment is arranged at a time convenient to the operator.

How do you obtain the Government's contribution?

At the end of each month you submit a voucher, as previously discussed. If the voucher is prepared properly, payment is usually made to you within two or three weeks.

Must you repay the Government the money it contributes?

You are required to pay royalty to the Government on any production from the land covered by the contract from the date of the contract until the Government notifies you, not later than six months after receipt of a sufficient final report, of certification or of its intent not to certify. If the Government considers that the exploration indicates that production may be possible from the area covered by the contract, it shall so certify. Thereafter, you must pay royalty on any subsequent production for the period specified in the contract. This royalty is five percent of the "gross proceeds" or the "value" of the production in the form in which it is sold, held, or used.

If a certification of possible production is made, how long do you pay royalty?

You pay royalty on production for a period of not less than 10 years and not more than 25 years from the date of the contract or until the Government's contribution is repaid with interest, whichever happens first.

Will you be required to pay royalty of the production of minerals not eligible for exploration assistance?

Yes, all minerals or metals produced or mined will be subject to the repayment provisions of the contract.

What security other than your legal obligation to pay does the Government have for payment of this royalty?

The contract gives the Government a lien on your land and on any production from it. The lien or subordination agreement affords the Government additional security.

Suppose the Government does not issue a certification of possible production? Then will the property be free from the Government's claim for royalty and the liens to secure its payment?

Yes, except with respect to any production that may occur during the time in which the Government has a right to certify, but not after the Government has given notification of its intent not to certify.

If the Government certifies that production may be possible, are you required to start producing?

No, you're the boss. The exploration contract does not require you to produce.

If you are a lessee of the property and your leasehold is surrendered to the owners, does this action destroy the Government's liens?

No, if you are a lessee, the lien agreement you procured from the owner establishes a lien on the land and any production from it. You also remain liable as surety for royalty on any production.

If your interest in the property is subject to a mortgage and the mortgage is foreclosed, does this foreclosure destroy the Government's liens?

No, the liens are protected by the subordination agreement you secured from the mortgagee. In this case, too, your liability as surety remains in effect.

Who pays the royalties to the Government?

If you sell your production, the purchaser should be notified of the Government's royalty interest and directed to make the payment to the Government, supporting the payment with copies of the settlement sheet. If the purchaser does not pay the royalty, you are liable for payment and must supply copies of settlement sheets or sales invoices.

How is the amount of the royalty verified?

This is done by audit of production records, sales amounts, and settlement sheets.

Does the Government charge interest on its contribution?

Simple interest is calculated from the first day of the month following the dates of the Government's contribution. Interest continues until the period for royalty payments expires as specified in the contract, or until the amount of the Government's contribution is fully repaid, whichever comes first.

What is the interest rate?

The rate, stated in the contract, is no less than the rate the Department of the Interior would be required to pay if it borrowed from the Treasury, plus a two percent interest charge in lieu of the actual cost to the Government of administering the contract.

How is the interest paid?

Interest is paid from the royalty on production. You are not obligated to pay unless you produce, and the interest does not increase the royalty rate.

If you transfer, surrender, or convey any of your rights in the land after certification, who becomes liable for the royalty?

You remain liable for the royalty on all production until the royalty period expires or the Government's contribution is fully repaid with interest.

What Federal Laws and Regulations must you comply with if a contract is granted?

You must comply with the following: Nondiscrimination in Employment, Work Hours Act of 1962 (Overtime Compensation), and the Copeland Anti-Kickback Act (Nonrebate of wages).

OFFICE OF MINERALS EXPLORATION
FIELD OFFICES

Region 1

Room 656
West 920 Riverside Ave.
Spokane, Wash. 99201

Includes Idaho, Montana, Oregon, and Washington.

Region 2

Building 2
345 Middlefield Road
Menlo Park, Calif. 94025

Includes Alaska, California, Nevada, and Hawaii

Region 3

Room 203, Building 53
Denver Federal Center
Denver, Colo. 80225

Includes Arizona, Colorado, Kansas, Nebraska,
New Mexico, North Dakota, Oklahoma, South Dakota,
Texas, Utah, and Wyoming.

Region 4

Room 11, Post Office
Building
Knoxville, Tenn. 37902

Includes all other States.

For additional information, write to the Office of Minerals Exploration, U.S. Geological Survey, Washington, D.C. 20242.

Chapter Ten

GRUBSTAKING, LEASING, OR SELLING

GRUBSTAKING, TODAY ACTUALLY a tenants-in-common undertaking, is as old as prospecting and is so well established an arrangement that in such a state as California the signed agreements must be recorded. In fact, most of the trouble that has arisen from grubstaking has not been so much a matter of dishonesty on the part of either party, but rather a lack of prior clear understanding of the terms.

For instance, you're ready to put your time and effort into prospecting for gold, but you're short of funds. Another interested individual, with money, agrees to buy your outfit and food and, these days probably, to advance you a small amount of money for other expenses. In return he becomes your partner, likely on a fifty-fifty basis. Half of anything you find, therefore, becomes his. Many mines in the past, particularly gold mines, have been started as a result of such an arrangement.

Up in Whitney-Tisdale townships by Ontario's Porcupine Lake, for example, a rich find of gold was filling the area with prospectors. Well in the van of this new rush were Benny Hollinger, a young barber, and Alex Gillies, both in Haileybury where they were trying to get grubstakes. Gillies had to be very persuasive to get $100 from Jack Miller. Hollinger was even less successful and had to be satisfied with $45 from Jack McMahon. Even then, McMahon thought so little of the gamble that he sold a half interest in his share for $55 to Gilbert Labine. The outcome of these grubstaking arrangements was that, although they went out as a team, the two prospectors were representing different backers.

They found an abandoned test pit where Reuben D'Aigle had left a rusting anvil and forge three years before. How narrowly D'Aigle had missed a fortune was revealed when a later assay of the gold in a sample they took from the bottom of the hole ran $52 a ton. Success struck on the second day after they had started to stake claims on the basis of some apparently unexceptional discoveries.

"I was cutting a discovery post, and Benny was pulling the moss off the rocks a few feet away," said Gillies, "when suddenly he let a roar out of him and threw his hat to me. At first I thought he was crazy, but when I came over to where he was, it was not hard to find the reason. The quartz where he had taken off the moss looked as though someone had dripped a candle along it, but instead of wax it was gold. The quartz stood up about three feet out of the ground and was about six feet wide, with gold all spattered over it and for about sixty feet along the vein."

They at once staked a dozen claims adjoining the discovery, along with an additional one for an old friend and former partner, Barney McEnany, who was no longer physically able to take to the wilderness. This claim later became the nucleus of the Porcupine Crown mine.

Now, because of their different grubstakers, Hollinger and Gillies had to decide how to split up the 12 claims. They tossed a coin. Hollinger won and picked the half-dozen claims on the west, thus laying the foundation for the tremendous Hollinger mine which was one of this continent's all-time greatest gold producers.

Once back in Haileybury, Hollinger and his sponsor McMahon, already ten dollars richer because of his deal with Gilbert Labine, talked over the situation with Alphonse Pare, a young McGill mining student who was a nephew of Noah Timmins. Timmins, an erstwhile Ontario storekeeper who had earlier made a fortune from the La Rosa mine at Cobalt, decided to follow Pare's opinion and at once bought Hollinger's six claims for $300,000.

The six claims which Alex Gillies had staked for himself and Jack Miller were to become the Acme mine but only after they, too, came into the Hollinger empire. Gillies and Miller optioned the property to the M. J. O'Brien interests, also based in Cobalt. A test diamond-drilling program was started, and a bundle of the heavy core was handed to a young engineer to pack out for assay. The weight was so much that the youthful engineer decided to lighten his burden and so threw away everything that did not show a high quartz content. Therein he revealed his lack of practical experience, for subsequent tests revealed that a large part of the gold was in the wall-rock schist. The outcome was that the O'Briens let their option lapse, whereupon the property was promptly taken up by the Timmins partnership. The cumulative production of all the gold mines in the area exceeds $1½ billion by a wide margin.

MONEY MEN

Sufficient capital for developing a mining property, and bringing it into production, is essential to the success of the operation. A common cause of mining failures is under-financing. The costs of exploration and development are extremely high these days. Extensive drilling is frequently necessary, and diamond drilling costs range from $7 to $20 a foot, while churn drillings run from $7 to $12 a foot.

Once a commercial deposit is shown to exist, deep shafts may be necessary at costs of $200 to $600 a foot, or perhaps huge volumes of overburden may have to be removed before mining can begin. Such undertakings are normally beyond the financial resources of the average individual prospector. In such cases it is frequently to his advantage to turn the prospect over to an established mining organization for development. Both exploration and development are complex undertakings, too often beset with uncertainties and disappointments. A mining firm is often better equipped with technical help and financing to cope with the problems that may arise than is an individual or group of individuals.

In these connections of selling and leasing finds, "prospecting" is defined as the search for mineral deposits, "exploration" as the determination of grade and tonnage of a newly found deposit, and "development" as the preparation of the deposit for mining. In readying a prospect for sale or lease the prospector is mainly concerned with exploration. A mineral deposit may be thought of as a marketable commodity. As such it has a market value that is dependent on the reserves of ore, the prevalent unit value of the commodity, and the grade of the deposit. If exploration increases the prospects of tonnage and grade, it also increases the market value.

Gold is one of the minerals that frequently can be profitably developed and mined by an individual or association of individuals, and requires little if any treatment to obtain a marketable product. With so many of such deposits already having been discovered and worked, such occurrences are becoming increasingly rare today.

If what seems to be an attractive property is repeatedly rejected by a number of concerns, it is likely because there are what look to be insufficient reserves to justify the capital expenditure necessary to bring the deposit into production. The owner must then either perform further speculative exploration in an effort to increase the known reserves or mine the prospect himself.

Some companies, especially the larger ones, are just not interested in properties in which the reserves are below what they consider to be a minimum figure, no matter what the grade. If existing exploration does not indicate reserves in the quantities dictated by the company policy, and there is little geologic evidence that further exploration will increase the outlook for reserves, an examining engineer will likely turn down the property even though the grade may be excellent. If the engineer's analysis is correct, the prospector may choose to mine the property himself on a small scale.

Before he takes such a step, however, he should be certain that the find is being displayed to its best advantage and that there is in fact insufficient possibility of increasing reserves by further exploration. He should also make as sure as possible that he has offered the property to companies most likely to be interested in it. Some concerns are more willing than others to take on small tonnage operations.

Extended exploration and development funds are what is regarded as risk or venture capital. In any business undertaking the greater the risk, the higher the cost of financing. Mining ventures are inherently more risky than most other types of business endeavors. The realtor, the lumberman, and the manufacturer can visually inspect and evaluate his product or its component parts, but the mining company representative can at best make only educated estimates of what lies beneath the surface. The product in toto is not visible and available for inspection.

The engineer or geologist bases his estimates on what he can see and what his experience with similar prospects has been. The prospector himself can do a great deal toward making his property attractive by performing exploration that will bring out the facts necessary for an accurate appraisal, at the least cost, of the deposit's potential. The prospector can expect to be repaid for work that increases the market value of the deposit.

Conversely, work done on long range projects such as mining facilities are often of no value to a buyer, and the prospector may feel he is not being fairly repaid for his efforts. Because a company necessarily evaluates work done by the prospector in relation to market value, exploration should be very carefully planned.

To this end a geologic map can be invaluable, and as new details are learned they should be added to the map, exploration plans being revised if necessary in light of new information. When possible the advice of a competent engineer or geologist should be sought in laying out exploration plans. Maximum information must be obtained for every dollar spent. The prospector should endeavor to bring out the promising features of the deposit in order to get the best price for his efforts. To this end the following points should be kept in mind:

1. Avoid Work Not Directed Toward Increasing Ore Reserves

After he is satisfied that there are economic quantities of ore, a buyer will prefer to solve in his own way many of the problems encountered on the long road from discovery to production. In general, a company will object to paying for mining facilities, long cross-cuts in barren ground to intersect ore at depth, haulage roads, and similar undertaking that do not increase the market value.

Only when a property is being sold as an equipped mine, fully developed and ready for production, will such items be worthwhile. Many long-range plans are laid out as exploration continues, and they are constantly revised as new data comes to light. A prospector with limited funds should concentrate on developing as much ore as possible with the least possible expenditure. In Alaska, for instance, under proper circumstances and when a private consultant cannot be obtained, Division of Mines and Geology personnel may visit a prospect and advise on an exploration plan.

Trenching, drilling, sampling, and underground work can all increase the market value of a deposit. Initial work, though, should be restricted to the more promising parts of the deposit. If funds prove to be available, further work can be extended into marginal areas.

2. Keep Track of Details

Sample locations should be clearly marked and sketch maps kept up to date to show where the samples were taken. Information should be included concerning the type of sample. The sample width is important, and the assay results are of course essential. Keep in mind that assay reports unsupported by specific information as to how and where a sample was collected will be discarded by a company seeking accurate information. The name of the assaying firm is of interest, and it is best to use the services of competent, industry-recognized assayers.

Drilling programs may be needed to prove the existence of adequate tonnages of ore. Drill holes, then, should have a definite purpose and target. Both the location and the direction of each hole should be the result of careful planning. The acquired information will be valuable only if careful and orderly logs of the holes are kept.

Cores, cuttings, and the like should be saved and labeled as to hole number and depth. When grade and tonnage are computed from corehole data the percentage of core recovery is an important factor. Accurate locations of all core holes should be determined. Here again, sketches showing locations of holes should be made if at all possible. Sketches of sections along the lengths of holes are also meaningful.

Trenches and pits are used to expose ore at the surface. Maps showing accurate locations of the excavations, along with sketches of individual trenches or pits, will add to the value of the work. Aerial photos can be useful as maps when enlarged, or they can be used as the base for an overlay. Aerial photographs may be ordered from the U.S. Geological Survey or other Federal agencies.

3. Decide How Much Work Can Be Afforded and Concentrate Effort

Once he decides to sell or lease his property the owner may decide to accept an increasing portion of the risk for an increasing portion of the benefit. From a company viewpoint, purchasing a completely unexplored property entails maximum risk, so the purchase price must be held to a small percentage of the probably total cost of the project.

Purchasing a developed mine with blocked-out ore rates a premium price because the owner has taken some or most of the risk himself. The negotiations will revolve around the value of the ore, the possibilities of extending the ore reserves, possible changes in the market for the ore, and the location of the deposit in regard to transportation facilities.

The safest approach to offering a mineral property for sale is to stake the claim and to put down a few drill holes or trenches in what seem to be the most favorable spots. The prospector will then not have assumed a great deal of financial risk. Hence, the purchase price will be a matter of the reward the prospector is entitled to for making the discovery and for a small amount of follow-up work.

If the prospector feels the prospect is such that he wants to accept additional risk in order to be in line for a greater return, he may go a few steps further. The procedure will be most applicable to the discovery of a high grade, easily developed deposit where they are geologic indications of large reserves.

Then the first steps would be to expose additional ore by pitting, underground work, or drilling. The work should be concentrated in highly mineralized areas, with only a scattering of pits and drill holes in the fringe regions. If this additional work is successful, the expected profit from the sale or lease of the property will be increased. Conversely, risk has also been increased for the owner. His money and work may have been expended in proving the ore body to be too small or of limited potential.

If the prospector decides to sell the prospect as a developed property with blocked-out ore, he must be careful not to exceed the point of diminishing returns, so as to keep the investment in line with the ultimate asking price. Certain items like used equipment or unusable development are likely to be considered valueless extras by a concern interested in purchasing the mine.

4. Be Specific and Give All the Facts

In presenting a mining prospect to a company it is well to be specific and candid about location, accessibility, and potential size. Enthusiasm and optimism are expected, but it is very important not knowingly to overestimate size and grade. A company representative who has traveled many miles to see a "tremendous" deposit is not likely to be very enthusiastic about a small pit with a few stains and will view any further representations by the prospector with suspicion.

It is a good idea when possible to have a report prepared by a reliable consultant. Competent mining engineers are generally registered. Geologists do not have a registration procedure, but checking with other prospectors and miners will in many cases reveal their competency. The report should include maps, photos, assay data, and an estimate of the ore reserves. There should be a clear statement about the method used to calculate the reserves and how far the ore is projected.

In Alaska if a prospector cannot afford a consultant, an engineer or geologist of the Division of Mines and Geology can visit the property to advise the owner on at least some of these points. Evidence must first be submitted to the Division indicating that the prospect has commercial possibilities. When warranted, sampling can be done and a report prepared.

If an owner gets together a report on his property, it should reasonably include enough pertinent data to interest an investor. Such items as the following may well be included:

a. Name of property and type of mineral.

b. Location, principal drainage basin, recording district, section, township, and survey quadrangle.

c. Clear directions for reaching the property from the nearest town, plus the best time of the year for travel there. If a regional map showing the property location is available, it should be included.

d. The names and addresses of all the people who have an interest in the property. The property's legal status, including the type and number of claims and leases. Any unsettled litigation that may involve the property, or questions concerning rightful ownership, should be settled before a property is offered for sale. Companies tend to shun properties in which there are title difficulties or hints of legal entanglements. Any liens or mortgages should also be noted at this time.

e. Note history and past production if applicable, as well as the history and past production of any similar nearby properties.

f. Bibliography of any reports that contain information on the property or the area. Mention individuals who would have knowledge of the deposit, such as a government geologist.

g. Give a brief description of the geology, mineralogy, and the deposit itself. Regarding this latter, mention the rock, apparent grade, length, width, possible depth, whether placer or lode, and whether it is massive or disseminated. Discuss exploration work to date, its results, and the further exploration that may be required to prove the ultimate potential.

h. Comment on possible mining methods and whether a surface or underground operation would be feasible in your opinion. This is not to say, of course, that the company may not proceed in an entirely different manner.

i. State the type of deal considered, whether outright sale or lease.

j. If the proposition has been turned down by another concern, this need not be mentioned unless the present prospect definitely inquires about it.

5. Have the Property Ready for Inspection

A company representative will be more likely to spend time on a property where the critical portion is accessible. A caved shaft, reported to be in ore, offers little encouragement. Neither does a trench or pit full of water or loose debris that masks the rock that is in place. Promising assays of samples from unmarked localities are discouraging to the examining engineer or geologist who may want to check samples.

All legal documents pertaining to the property such as partnership agreement, claim records, and the like should be available. A claim map and a base map will be helpful.

The prospector should keep in mind that even if the company representative may reject the site, the geologist or engineer may express unofficial opinions and recommendations that are likely to be helpful in deciding upon the next course of action.

For his own protection, it is best for the prospector to have properly documented legal locations or a definite interest in a property before he shows it to a possibly interested party. This is not to imply that the company in question may not be trustworthy, but individuals have human frailties, and such a safeguard may save embarrassment, misunderstandings, or hard feelings in the future. Legal documents include location and discovery notices, proofs of development work, quit claim deeds, and the like.

6. Consider the Company's Position When a Property is Being Examined

The prospector in many instances may feel that a property examination by a company representative was too hasty. The engineer may reject it after a brief look, or he may decide to return later, especially if the initial examination was in the nature of a reconnaissance. Remember that the property is in competition with other prospects for company exploration dollars.

The engineer may be on a trip during which he plans to examine a number of possibilities. From these he will select perhaps one or two that seem to offer the best profit potential. If he rejects the property upon an initial look, he may have seen others that are more attractive. If he decides to return later, it could be that he wants to make a thorough examination and that time for the work must be scheduled.

To a property owner who has spent months or years working on a prospect, it is especially frustrating to have it turned down after a look of no more than a few brief hours. This is understandable. The earnest prospector deserves encouragement rather than discouragement. However, a mine examination is merely a process of testing the successive links of a chain of observed facts. As soon as any link is found that is too weak for the entire purpose, the examination is over. Any further survey confuses the issue and wastes the client's money.

The company geologist thinks in terms of potential profits. However, the requirements of the particular company at the moment are also considerations. A small, high-grade deposit may not be what the enterprise is looking for at the particular time. A large deposit that cannot begin to produce for a long time may be a good investment, but it may not fit the concern's immediate needs.

If there are good indications that the prospect will make a paying mine, with continued effort an interested company can generally be found. An attractive property may be turned down because of transportation difficulties, because of a purchase price that seems too big for the risk involved, or because of seemingly unreasonable demands in regard to the time permitted for exploration.

The examining geologist or engineer is entrusted with the responsibility of investing his employer's money. He must earn the respect of management and merit the confidence placed in his decision. The agent is apt to be much more conservative than the mine owner when it comes to projecting ore bodies. This conservatism stems from the fact that he must weigh one property against another and determine where his firm's capital may be invested to its greatest advantage.

Even when the agent is sufficiently impressed to deal, his report and recommendation are scrutinized by other geologists, engineers, and management personnel. A favorable recommendation may be reversed for any number of reasons on any rung of the corporate ladder.

The majority of mining companies are naturally hesitant to take long chances on undeveloped ground unless the economic potential is decidedly great enough to justify the risk. A decision to gamble on a property that shows little geologic encouragement is best left to the investor looking for a tax write-off or to one whose principal source of income is not from mining. Admittedly, such speculations have paid off famously at times.

CONTACTS

If your prospect is in Alaska, the Division of Mines and Geology there, being familiar with many interested mining companies, can often put a prospector in touch with money men most likely to be interested in the particular type of property. The governor's office even maintains an office in Tokyo where contacts with Japanese firms are made.

Then there are the professional agents and promoters who perform highly necessary services in the mining industry. For instance, a property owner who does not have the contacts to bring his prospect to the attention of likely buyers may well wish to work through an agent. Before such a deal is entered into, though, the commissions involved should be clearly stated and understood.

Mine promotion, too, is a legitimate business. When an owner attempts to sell a property he often faces problems in fields where he is totally inexperienced. An arrangement with a reputable mine promoter may then often be advantageous to both, the promoter for his part contributing knowledge and experience as well as time and effort to press the project forward.

The promoter may work for a finder's fee or for an actual interest in the property. In some instances, the promoter will lease the prospect from the owner and in turn sublease it to a mining company.

EXPLORATION AGREEMENTS AND OPTIONS

Before a mining company will expend important funds on a property it will require time to examine the prospect thoroughly and to prepare engineering and geology reports. The concern may be willing to discuss the broad outlines of a deal or to enter into an exploration agreement on a short-term basis. Such an agreement will likely contain an option to proceed to a more formal lease or purchase arrangement by a certain deadline.

Exploration leases and purchase agreements are commonly used in the mining industry. A lease is normally drawn up with an option that gives the company the right to buy at a specified figure and at set terms. The company, in turn, agrees to perform a certain amount of work while the lease is running, and it will usually be prepared to furnish the owner with copies of the results obtained. It will be to the owner's advantage, ordinarily, to give the company time to do a good exploration job. However, provisions for certain work to be done within a specified time should be included, although provisions for time extensions are not unusual.

It is not customary for a company to make a cash payment at the outset of an exploration lease, although there are exceptions as when there is a sellers' market and also when the owner has incurred many debts and liabilities in exploring or in tying up a prospect.

PURCHASE AGREEMENTS

Any number of purchase arrangements are possible, but there are three basic types; an outright cash deal, lease and bond, and participation. Much of the deal depends on the personal preference of the seller and on the company policy, but also important are the nature and characteristics of the deposit, the financial position of both the concern and the prospector, and the amount of money involved. A management contract or a stock interest arrangement are other types of deals, less commonly used.

a. Outright Cash Purchase

Unless a company feels that the price is a bargain for an unusually attractive proposition, it will not favor an outright cash purchase. If the outfit does agree to a cash deal, the purchase price is usually paid over a number of years, commonly three to five. The buyer ordinarily reserves the right to terminate the agreement at any time without being committed to additional payments.

b. Lease and Bond

This is the most common arrangement between buyers and sellers of mining properties. A final price is established, usually when an exploration lease is initiated. Minimum payments are stipulated to extend regularly over a period of time until the full purchase price is met.

These payments are typically royalty fees on production, either at set rates or on a sliding scale determined by the grade of ore mined. Royalty payments may exceed the stipulated minimum payment. On the other hand, there is no provision that the payments must continue if the company finds the mine unprofitable. In this unfortunate event, both lease and bond are cancelled, and the property with all improvements reverts to the owner.

As an example of how a company may negotiate for the prospect whose size and value are unknown, an agreement to lease is reached which may or may not contain a purchase option. Work commitments and minimum royalties vary with each property, production royalties usually being one of the following:

1. Ten percent of net smelter returns until the owner has received $35,000, which prevents the company from high-grading a deposit the prospector has developed.

2. Seven-and-one-half percent of net smelter returns until the owner has received $75,000.

3. Five percent of net smelter returns until the owner has received $200,000.

4. Two-and-one-half percent of net smelter returns until the owner has received $1 million or $1\frac{1}{4}\%$ for as long as the property produces.

Features 2 and 3 are for ore developed by the company that is probably a continuation of ore discovered by the prospector. Feature 4 is applied to large low-grade deposits and helps compensate the company for the high capital investment that is usually required in such instances.

The company prefers to establish a final purchase price toward which all royalties or other payments apply.

If the seller insists on what are regarded as unduly high royalties, the company may high-grade the deposit in order to make a profit. Furthermore, it may decide that capital cannot be expended on exploration to lengthen the life of the mine.

Some companies may wish to make initial payments through a transfer of stock in lieu of cash. Whether to accept this method of recompense depends on the individual preferences and circumstances of the property owner.

c. Participation

Under a participation agreement the company stipulates to spend a certain amount of money in a specified time to accomplish a certain result. That is, it may agree to engage in an extended drilling campaign of a stated number of feet, or to sink a shaft to a specified depth, or to build a mill of a determined minimum capacity, or to perform a set amount of underground work.

This work could involve a series of steps, each depending on the success of the one preceding. Such an arrangement would probably be more applicable to a partly developed mine than to a prospect.

The company will almost always insist on full management control. The equity retained by the seller is variable, often ranging between 10% and 50%. Participation contracts usually contain a provision for the company to recover its capital investment off the top; that is, before any division of profits.

In contrast to the lease and bond arrangement, the participation agreement just described is less advantageous to the seller in that he may have to wait a long time to share in any profits. However, if the mine has an extended life, his total gain may be greater.

Other types of participation agreements include stock option plans, escrowed shares, free shares, and senior financing arrangements. Such plans may be worked out to enable the seller to receive negotiable securities that may be sold before a profit is made, thus overcoming the difficulty of not sharing in the profits for a long time if the company must first recover a large capital investment.

MANAGEMENT CONTRACTS AND STOCK INTERESTS

If the seller desires to maintain an interest or equity in a property but is disinterested in actively participating in management, he may find that a management contract may be advantageous. The company agrees to operate the mine for a fee. The fee may be a portion of the profits or a fixed charge. This arrangement is usually more applicable to a producing mine, or to one that has been developed to the point of production, than to an undeveloped prospect.

Another type of agreement involves the prospector's accepting an interest in a public or private company which may be set up to develop the property. The prospector would be entitled to an interest in the property, which would be defined in the agreement and might amount to a 25% nonparticipating share. The company developing the prospect usually acquires an increasing interest proportional to the funds expended. For example, an expenditure of $10 million might give the concern a 70% interest, whereas a $15 million outlay would possibly entitle it to a 75% share.

YUKON AND NORTHWEST TERRITORIES

The Prospectors' Assistance Program is designed to encourage the search for gold and other minerals in the Yukon and Northwest Territories. The Department of Indian Affairs and Northern Development, Ottawa, Ontario, will supply funds to finance the individual enterprises.

The plan, briefly, is that a prospector may receive financial assistance up to $900 per fiscal year to help finance his prospecting venture in the Yukon or Northwest Territories. The amount of help a prospector may get is determined by the following formula:

Total assistance for food, rental of equipment, and expendable items shall not exceed $350. The remainder, up to $550, is to offset traveling expenses in the field. This may be used for air charter, rental of vehicles, boats, pack horses, etc. If a prospector uses his own vehicle, boat, or airplane, the normal operating costs may be charged against this allotment by supplying vouchers, or he may apply approved rental rates on a per mile basis which must be approved by the Prospectors' Assistance Board.

An advance of up to two-thirds of the approved assistance may be given the prospector at the beginning of the season and the remainder paid after the individual has completed his field work to the satisfaction of the Review Committee.

It is recognized that transportation by aircraft is the major item of cost to prospectors in northern Canada. In order to maintain control of airplane travel and to equalize benefits for prospectors working in more remote areas from main centers of transportation, approval for air travel may be granted only as follows:

(a) one trip into the area at the beginning of the season to establish the base camp. The point of origin of the trip is left to the discretion of the Prospectors' Assistance Board. It must not be outside the Territories unless it is cheaper for the prospector to establish his base camp from a point elsewhere;

(b) one trip back to the point of origin at the end of the season; and

(c) one service trip per month from the nearest convenient settlement or source of supply to the prospector's base camp.

In case of travel by motor vehicle, a rate of 12c a mile will be allowed, but under no circumstances will an amount exceeding that calculated above under (a), (b), and (c) be approved.

In addition to the monetary aid, prospectors will also be supplied on request without charge with:

(a) one safety flare kit with 12 emergency flares;

(b) topographic maps, claim maps, and aerial photographs for the area he will be prospecting. When air photos are requested, prospectors are reminded to allow sufficient time to obtain these from the Air Photographic Library;

(c) fifteen assays during the fiscal year, provided that such assays are made within the Yukon or Northwest Territory when an assay office is available there. In the case of prospectors working in the Arctic and Hudson Bay Mining District where it is more practical to send assays to laboratories in eastern Canada, the cost of assaying may be charged against the program but the cost of sending the samples out will be the responsibility of the prospector.

The fiscal year begins on 1 April and ends on 31 March in the following year. Prospecting may be conducted at any time during the fiscal year for both placer and lode deposits.

Any prospector who is able to show the Prospectors' Assistance Board that he is capable and sufficiently well equipped to go into the field on a prospecting venture may apply for financial assistance under the program. However, any one gravel puncher will receive assistance in only one of the two Territories in any one fiscal year. Applicants must be at least 21 years old and must satisfy the Board that they have a sound knowledge of prospecting techniques and are able to survive in the wilderness. They may also be required to pass a simple test on mineral identification. Incidentally, underage individuals may receive assistance provided they are to work with an experienced applicant.

Applications for assistance should be made as soon as possible after the beginning of the fiscal year, but they may also be accepted at any time during the fiscal year for which assistance is requested. Although applications will be approved on an individual basis, there is no objection to two or more prospectors working as a team and pooling their assistance.

Prospectors must spend a minimum of 60 days prospecting within the territories during the fiscal year in which assistance is requested, although in very exceptional cases they may receive partial assistance if unable to complete the 60 days in the field due to reasons beyond their control.

Prospectors are required to disclose in advance to the Board, on a confidential basis, where their camps will be established. If they move from one area to another, they must inform the Board of any change in camp location in order that they may be found during inspection trips.

The emphasis should be placed on the search for new showings. Assistance, however, may be given a prospector who is exploring a mineral occurrence on claims which he has recorded while participating in this, or previous, Prospectors' Assistance Programs.

Prospectors must keep daily diaries of their activities and include sketches and maps showing mineral occurrences, location of trenches and drill holes, or any other type of physical work performed. At the end of the season, the diary will be submitted to the Review Committee along with maps, sketches, and any other pertinent information. All such submissions by prospectors must be in the hands of the Review Committee by 1 March of the fiscal year for which assistance is claimed. The diaries themselves will be supplied by the Board.

Prospectors may stake mineral claims at their own expense during the period of assistance, and the Government will not claim any interest or ownership in these claims.

SASKATCHEWAN

The Department of Mineral Resources in Regina, Saskatchewan started in 1972 a Prospectors' Incentive Plan, designed to encourage the active participation of native and other northern residents in mineral exploration and development in northern Saskatchewan. In addition to training interested inhabitants of the north through provincial prospectors schools, this program is carried out by supporting them in active prospecting and claim staking in northern Saskatchewan.

Prospecting teams participating in the Plan are placed in areas selected on the basis of favorable geology and structure and/or known mineralization, as well as occasionally in districts where mineral occurrences have been observed previously by the prospector while engaged in other activities such as trapping, fishing, and hunting.

Any resident of northern Saskatchewan, interested in prospecting, is eligible to participate. Application should be made to the Director, Prospectors' Incentive Plan, Department of Northern Saskatchewan, La Ronge, Sask. Under the Plan, however, it is required that the individual agrees to prospect with a partner whom he himself selects. Occasionally, where a large area can be prospected from one central location, it becomes more economical for four or more prospectors to work out of one main camp. It is considered desirable, in fact, to have more than one party working in a particular region because servicing single parties becomes excessively costly.

Under the P.I.P. agreement the prospector is paid a monthly wage while in the field and is provided with all necessary field equipment, sustenance, and transportation. Should a mineral discovery be made which merits exploration, on the advice of the Minister or his qualified representative, the ground will be staked on behalf of the Department of Northern Saskatchewan.

When exploration which includes one or more geological, geochemical, and geophysical surveys is carried out, a cash bonus totaling $1,000 is paid to the prospector or prospectors making the discovery. When diamond drilling is conducted to test the discovery, a cash bonus of 50 cents per foot up to 2,000 feet of drilling, and 25c per foot thereafter to a total bonus not exceeding $50,000, shall be paid to the prospector or prospectors over a period of seven years or less from the date of discovery.

If a producing mine is established on the discovery area, the prospector or prospectors are entitled to one percent of the value of the ore at the mouth of the mine, as determined by the Minister. When more than one individual is involved in the discovery, the bonus and the royalty paid on the ore mined will be shared proportionately.

An agreement has also been drawn up for the free lance prospector who does not wish to participate in the Prospectors' Incentive Plan. Under this agreement, the individual is neither paid a wage while prospecting nor provided with equipment, food, and transportation. However, if in the opinion of a qualified representative of the Department of Northern Saskatchewan a discovery has been made, an agreement may be negotiated whereby the Province acquires the property for a certain amount if it is staked, and if it is open ground, it will be staked on behalf of the Department of Northern Saskatchewan. From that stage of negotiation, the finder or finders would be eligible to receive the same cash bonuses and royalty on ore mined as under the P.I.P.

BRITISH COLUMBIA

Grubstakes up to a maximum of $500 for food, shelter, and clothing, plus a reasonable traveling allowance, are available to a limited number of qualified prospectors who undertake to prospect in British Columbia in areas considered favorable in accordance with a long-range plan for the development of the Province. A limited number of experienced prospectors may be granted a maximum of $300 for traveling expenses where prospecting is to be carried on in remote areas where air transportation is deemed necessary.

Items such as guns, fishing gear, stoves, boats, and outboard motors are not considered as legitimate charges against the grant and must be provided by the applicant. However, a reasonable rental charge may be considered for necessities such as horses and pack saddles.

The grant is usually given in two payments by the British Columbia Department of Mines and Petroleum Resources, Victoria, B.C. The initial payment is made at the start of the season and the second after either a report has been received from the field supervisor or the grantee has completed 60 days of prospecting. Applications should be submitted by 30 April.

Unless the applicant has been previously grubstaked and found to be competent, it will be necessary for him to pass a simple test of his ability to identify hand specimens of rocks and minerals commonly found in the Province. He must be a British subject between the ages of 18 and 70 years and must have been resident in B.C. during the year preceding the date of application. He should have bush experience and be physically and mentally fit. He must be a bona fide prospector holding an unexpired Free Miner's Certificate.

Grubstakes will be granted only on the understanding that the grantee spend at least 60 days in the field actually prospecting and that he will not accept any pay for services rendered during that period from any other source. If he is unable to comply with these requirements, he agrees to return a part of the grubstake funds proportional to the part of the 60 days not spent prospecting. Time taken in traveling to and from the prospecting area, as well as days taken off from prospecting, are not included in the stipulated 60 days.

As far as is reasonably practicable, the field season should consist of continuous prospecting until the terms and conditions of the grubstake have been completed. Time out is permitted during inclement weather, illness, or for securing necessary supplies. The grubstakes are not intended for weekend prospecting or for short trips from a home base.

The prospector is required to keep a diary and to plot the area worked, doing this latter on a suitable map. The possible importance of the samples submitted for free assay can be better determined if descriptions, particularly as to the extent of the mineralization, are recorded in the diary. The completed diary must be submitted to the Department at the end of the prospecting season. When two or three prospectors are working together, one diary will be accepted for the group if it is signed by each partner.

Grubstakes are granted with the object of maintaining the search for mineral occurrences with mine-making possibilities. The grants are not intended for the purpose of exploring or developing mineral occurrences already found. One year only will be allowed for prospecting ground that has been staked by a prospector while on grubstake. Time will not be allowed for prospecting on old properties which have had work done on them, unless mineral occurrences of present economic importance have been discovered on them for the first time.

No interest is retained by the Government in any discovery made by a grantee other than that which applies in common with all Free Miners. Incidentally, in the granting of grubstakes, preference will be given to those applicants who have arranged to be accompanied in the field by one or two other prospectors. But such teaming up does not of itself constitute joint ownership of personal property or mining claims. If joint ownership is desired, it should be so stated in an appropriately prepared document signed by the participants. Such a document would be a mutual agreement between the members of a team and is not a condition in any way of the British Columbia grubstake program.

Chapter Eleven

STAKING ON FEDERAL LANDS

THE WORDS *claim* and *mining claim* have a precise meaning when used in connection with this country's mining laws, referring to a particular piece of land, valuable for specific minerals, to which an individual has asserted a right of possession for the purpose of developing and extracting discovered minerals. This right is granted the miner if he meets the requirements of the mining laws. These same laws guarantee him protection for all lawful uses of his claim for mining purposes. If the requirements of the law have not been met, however, no rights are granted.

JURISDICTION OVER MINING CLAIMS

The Bureau of Land Management, an agency of the U.S. Department of the Interior, has the primary responsibility for administering the laws and regulations governing the disposal of most minerals on public lands. Administering the U.S. mining laws so as to "promote the development of the mining resources of the United States" is one of that Bureau's objectives.

A so-called Memorandum of Understanding of April 1957, as amended, between the Bureau of Land Management and the Forest Service provides for cooperative procedures in the administration of the mining laws on National Forest System lands, even including the examination of mining claims in the National Forests by Forest Service inspectors.

A bill signed in 1971 by President Richard M. Nixon establishes as a continuing national policy the "need to foster and encourage private enterprise in (1) the development of economically sound and stable domestic mining, minerals, metals and mineral reclamation industries; (2) the orderly and economic development of domestic mineral resources, reserves, and reclamation of metals and minerals to help assure satisfaction of industrial and security needs; (3) mining, mineral, and metallurgical research, including the use and recycling of scrap; and (4) the study and development of methods for the disposal, control, and reclamation of mineral waste products, and the reclamation of mined land, so as to lessen any adverse impact of mineral extraction and processing upon the physical environment that may result from mining or mineral activities."

THE DIFFERENT LANDS

Federal lands are all lands owned by the Federal Government and administered by its agencies. This includes public domain lands and acquired lands.

Public domain lands are those which the United States acquired from Great Britain, Spain, Russia, and other countries as it expanded westward. Those lands still in Federal ownership and not reserved for specific purposes are administered by the Bureau of Land Management.

Acquired lands are areas in Federal ownership which were secured by the Government by purchase, gift, or condemnation. These properties are not open to location under the mining laws.

National Forest lands are Federal lands administered by the Forest Service, U.S. Department of Agriculture, and include both lands reserved from the public domain for National Forests and acquired areas.

ADMINISTRATION

The 420 million acres of public land under the jurisdiction of the Bureau of Land Management are handled under the numerous Public

Land laws, by multiple-use principles which insure their being managed for mining, grazing, timber production, recreation, wildlife, and other uses. The basic objective is to secure optimum benefits for the general public by managing and using all the resources of public areas for the best possible combination of resource advantages.

The 187 million acres of National Forest System lands, which include 27 million acquired acres, are administered by the Forest Service under the Organic Act of 1897 and the principles of the Multiple Use-Sustained Yield Act of 1960. This latter Act requires maintenance of recreation, timber, range, watersheds, and wildlife on a sustained yield basis without impairing the productivity of the property.

THE MINING LAWS

Congress passed in 1872 an Act to Promote the Development of the Mining Resources of the United States. If you wish to file a mining claim on public domain land open to location under the mining laws, this is the law giving you the right to do so. At the same time, it is the law setting the limits of your rights.

This mining law, together with the regulations and the court decisions which have interpreted them, are collectively called the General Mining Laws. These laws apply to all minerals except the so-called leasing act minerals such as oil, gas, coal, etc., common varieties of sand and gravel and the like, and petrified wood. Certain lands reserved from the public domain, discussed later, are withdrawn from location and entry.

WHEN SHOULD YOU STAKE A CLAIM?

A mining claim is for one purpose only—to permit the development and extraction of certain valuable mineral deposits. In other words, be sure a mining claim is neither a simple nor an inexpensive way of obtaining a piece of land. The requirements of the mining laws, especially as they are now interpreted, are not that easy to meet. Unless you are convinced you can meet them, a mining claim will not be what you are looking for.

If you wish land on which to build a house or summer cabin, a filling station, or an entire resort, staking a mining claim is not the way to obtain the property. If you are able to meet the requirements, there are other means such as purchase under other acts or through a special-use permit by which it may be possible to occupy land for personal, business, or recreational purposes.

MINERALS

A mineral by one definition is an inorganic homogenous substance occurring naturally as a part of the earth's crust and having a definite chemical composition. As used in the mining laws, however, a mineral is any substance recognized as a mineral by the standard authorities, whether metallic or some other substance, when found in public lands in quantity and quality sufficient to make the land valuable because of its presence.

Such minerals are of three types:

1. *Locatable*—Both metallic (gold, silver, platinum, etc.) and nonmetallic (asbestos, fluorspar, mica, and such) minerals may be located under the mining laws.

2. *Salable*—By law, certain materials may not be located under the mining regulations but may be purchased under the Materials Sales Act of 1947 at their fair market value, either at competitive or noncompetitive sales. These include the common varieties of sand, gravel, stone, pumice, cinders, pumicite, and even clay. Petrified wood is not subject to location under the mining laws. Small amounts, however, may be removed for noncommercial uses by hobbyists. Larger amounts may be bought.

3. *Leasable*—A few other minerals and fuels, although they may not be claimed under the mining laws, may be leased from the Government. These include oil, gas, shale, potash, sodium, phosphate, native asphalt, solid and semi-solid bitumen, bituminous rock, coal, phosphate and, in New Mexico and Louisiana, sulphur. On certain lands, such as acquired lands and offshore areas, all minerals are subject to special leasing regulations and laws.

WHAT IS A DISCOVERY OF VALUABLE MINERAL?

A mining claim may be validly located and held only after the discovery there of a valuable mineral deposit.

It is a common misunderstanding among prospectors that if they sink a discovery shaft or make other mining improvements, then put up their corner stakes or monuments to identify the land, they automatically acquire an interest in the land even though there may be absolutely no indication of valuable minerals within the claim. They also often believe, equally mistakenly, that the performance of annual assessment work will perpetuate their "right" to such a claim.

Regardless of the prevalence of this belief, according to the law such a location is worthless and no rights to the land have been established.

The courts have set up, and the Government follows, the prudent-man rule to determine what is the discovery of a valuable mineral. Under this rule, where minerals have been found and the evidence is of such a character that a person of ordinary prudence would be justified in further expenditure of his labor and means, with a reasonable prospect of success, in developing a valuable mine, the requirements of the statute have been met.

Economic factors such as market, cost versus returns, and so forth are important considerations in applying the prudent-man test. Too many individuals have misunderstood this to mean that merely any showing of a mineral, or a hope or wish for future discovery, is sufficient.

This is incorrect. There must be an actual physical discovery of the mineral on each and every mining claim and, furthermore, this discovery must satisfy the prudent-man rule. Traces, isolated bits of mineral, and other such minor indications are not enough to satisfy the prudent-man clause.

TYPES OF MINING CLAIMS

Mining claims are of four types:

1. *Lode claims*—Deposits subject to lode claims include classic veins or lodes having well-defined boundaries. Including other rock in place bearing valuable minerals, they may also be broad zones of mineralized rock. Examples include quartz and other veins carrying gold.

2. *Placer claims*—Deposits subject to placer claims are all those not coming under lode claims. These include the true placer deposits of sand and gravel containing free gold.

3. *Mill site*—A mill site is a plot of unappropriated public domain land of a nonmineral character, suitable for the erection of a mill or reduction works. Mill sites may be located under either of the following circumstances:

a. when used or occupied distinctly and explicitly for mining and milling purposes in connection with a lode or placer location with which it is associated.

b. for a quartz mill or reduction works unconnected with a mineral location.

4. *Tunnel site*—A tunnel site is located on a plot of land where a tunnel is run to develop a vein or lode, or to discover a vein or lode. Tunnel sites, incidentally, may not be patented.

CLAIM SHAPES AND SIZES

Lode claims are generally parallelograms, with longer side lines parallel to the vein or lode. They are located by metes and bounds, giving the length and direction of each boundary line. They are limited by statute to a maximum of 1,500 feet in length, along the vein or lode, and 300 feet on either side.

Placer claims, when practicable, are located by a legal subdivision; a legal subdivision being a part of a section, that is, NW 1/4 NW 1/4 Section 8, Township 7 North, Range 19 West, Willamette Meridian. They are limited to 20 acres per claim per locator. However, an association of two locators may stake 40 acres, three 60 acres, etc., the maximum being 160 acres for eight individuals. Each locator should have a bona fide interest in the claim lest he be considered a dummy locator and lose his rights. Corporations are limited to 20-acre claims. On unsurveyed land and in certain other instances, placer claims can be located by metes and bounds.

Mill sites are located by metes and bounds. They are limited in size to 5 acres per claim.

Tunnel sites are located by driving two stakes 3,000 feet apart on the line of the proposed tunnel. The miner may locate lode claims to cover any and all veins intersected by the tunnel. This, in essence, gives you the right to prospect in an area 3,000 feet by 3,000 feet.

WHERE TO PROSPECT IN THE U.S.

There are large areas, mainly in the western states, where you may prospect for minerals and, discovering a valuable deposit, stake a mining claim. These regions are in Alaska, Arizona, Arkansas, California, Colorado, Idaho, Montana, Nebraska, Nevada, New Mexico, North Dakota, Oregon, South Dakota, Utah, Washington, Wyoming, and certain parts of Florida, Louisiana, and Mississippi.

Such areas are mostly on open (not withdrawn) public domain land administered by the Forest Service of the Department of Agriculture or by the Bureau of Land Management of the Department of the Interior. You may also locate mining claims on certain patented lands in which the Government has reserved the mineral rights, although you may mine and patent only the reserved minerals in such lands. Care then must be taken to avoid damage to resources owned by others.

Although most of the public and the National Forest lands are open to prospecting under the mining law, the vast majority of the total acreage likely does not contain valuable minerals. The reason for prospecting is to determine where the regions holding valuable minerals are located. Only after such a discovery may you validly stake a mining claim.

RESTRICTIONS

The Government retains the right to manage the surface and the surface resources on most mining claims on National Forest lands, as prescribed in the Act of 23 July 1955.

Several acts of Congress have modified the General Mining Laws applicable to certain areas of National Forest land. In these localities the locater of a mining claim obtains only such rights as the law prescribes.

According to The Wilderness Act of 3 September 1964, the mining laws and mineral leasing laws apply to the National Forest lands designated by the Act as "Wilderness" until the end of 1983 to the same extent as they applied prior to 3 September 1964. Mining on these lands is subject to the provisions of the law and the wilderness regulations of the Secretaries of Agriculture and Interior. Current regulations may be learned from local Forest Service officers or Bureau of Land Management offices.

Regulations issued 31 May 1966 prescribe access to valid mining claims as well as to prospecting and mining operations. You should get in touch with a local Forest Service officer before entering a Wilderness. He will also provide you with a copy of the regulations and discuss them with you.

National Forest Primitive Areas are administered in the same manner as Wilderness.

Generally, the National Parks and most National Monuments are closed to mining, as are Indian reservations, the majority of reclamation projects, military reservations, scientific testing areas, some wildlife protection areas such as Federal game refuges, and lands segregated under the Classification and Multiple Use Act. Lands withdrawn for power purposes, though, are subject to location and entry under certain conditions.

Certain lands reserved from the public domain under the jurisdiction of the Forest Service and the Bureau of Land Management are also withdrawn from location and entry under the General Mining Laws by act of Congress or by public land order. No mining claims may be located on such lands as long as such withdrawal is in effect.

These closed areas are said to be "withdrawn" from mining location and entry. The public land records in the local Bureau of Land Management office will show you which public lands are withdrawn. It is important that you do not attempt to locate and remove minerals from these withdrawn lands. Not only would your work be wasted, but such activities would be a trespass against the Government and subject to penalties.

LOCATING A CLAIM

The essential elements in locating a gold claim are:

1. The physical exposure or discovery of gold.

2. Clearly and distinctly marking the boundaries of the claim on the ground so that the claim can be readily identified.

3. Posting the notice of location in a conspicuous spot, usually at the place of discovery.

4. Finally, the recording of an exact copy of the location in the appropriate office, usually the County Recorder's office in the county in which the claim is located. In Alaska, the recording office is under the District Magistrate. Claims in certain areas, as in parts of Oregon, must also be recorded with the Bureau of Land Management.

Except in Alaska, Federal mining law does not require a notice of location either to be posted or recorded. However, most individual states to which the mining laws apply have, by local statutes, required posting and recording. You should check state requirements carefully.

These requirements vary from state to state. Usually, however, a location notice must contain the following information:

a. date,

b. name of locator (s),

c. name of claim,

d. whether this is a placer or lode type,

e. the mineral claimed,

f. the distance claimed along the course of the vein, each way from the discovery point and the direction (for lode claims and placer claims located by metes and bounds), or the acreage claimed and the legal description by particular parts of the section, township, and range (for placer claims located by legal subdivisions),

g. a connection by distance and direction as accurately as practicable from the discovery point to some well-known, permanent, and prominent natural object or landmark such as a hill, mountain, bridge, fork of a stream, or road intersection. Where a placer claim is located by legal subdivision, no other tie-in is necessary.

MARKING YOUR CLAIM

Federal laws specify only that a claim should be marked distinctly enough to be readily identified. However, each state generally has detailed and different requirements for marking boundaries. As a minimum, ordinarily, all four corners of lode or placer claims, unless located by legal subdivision, should be marked with posts or stone monuments. The point of discovery of both lode and placer claims should be marked by a post or monument. The location notice, giving information about the claim, should be placed in or on this marker.

Such procedure identifies and establishes the boundaries of your claim and is notification to others of the claim. The more clearly the boundaries are marked and the stricter the state laws are adhered to, the less chance exists of your claim being jumped; that is, appropriated by others.

RECORDING YOUR CLAIM

Each state has established its own detailed procedures for receiving and recording location notices. These notices are generally filed with

the County Recorder's office in the county in which the find has been made and in Alaska with the District Magistrate.

Location notices are not filed with the Bureau of Land Management except in a few instances where this is specifically required by law. In these situations, copies must also be filed in the usual place for recordings as specified by state law.

With any claim located in a National Forest Wilderness, the Forest Supervisor or District Ranger having jurisdiction over the land must be notified in writing within 30 days after the date of location.

MAINTAINING YOUR CLAIM

At least $100 worth of labor or improvements must be performed on, or for the benefit of the claim each and every year. Called annual assessment work, this must be completed on or before noon on 1 September of each year. Proving your active interest in the claim, it must be done to protect your right against jumping or location by others.

You should follow up this assessment work by filing in the County Recorder's or other office each year a statement with the Bureau of Land Management except where otherwise specifically required by law.

The assessment requirement can be fulfilled, incidentally, by conducting geological, geophysical, and geochemical surveys. These must be handled by qualified experts and verified by a report filed in the county or recording district office in the area where the claim is located. Such a report must fully set forth the following:

1. The location of the work in relation to the point of discovery and the claim boundaries.

2. Nature, extent, and cost of the work.

3. The fundamental findings of the surveys.

4. The name, address, and professional standing of the person or persons who have done the work.

Surveys of this sort may not be applied as labor for more than two consecutive years or for more than a total of five years on any single mining claim. Each survey must be nonrepetitive. Furthermore, surveys of this sort will not apply toward the statutory provision that necessitates the expenditure of $500 for each claim for mineral patent.

Incidentally, there is the loophole that after failure to perform the annual assessment work, the work may be resumed if this is done before someone else relocates the claim.

WHAT ABOUT STATE MINING LAWS?

The United States mining laws are supplemented in most areas by state statutes. These statutes specify such things as the manner of locating a claim, marking the boundaries, recording notices of location and annual assessment work, the size of discovery pits and shafts, and so on. As these laws and requirements vary from jurisdiction to jurisdiction, you should request additional information from the local state offices to be on the safe side.

HOW MANY CLAIMS?

There is no limit to the number of claims you may hold so long as you have made a discovery of a valuable mineral and met other requirements on each one. Only one discovery of mineral is needed to support a placer claim, no matter if it is 20 acres for you, yourself, or up to 160 acres for a group of people.

WHO MAY STAKE A CLAIM?

Anyone who's a U.S. citizen, or who has declared his intention of becoming a citizen, may stake or locate a mining claim in this country. This includes both miners who are bona fide locators and corporations organized under the laws of any state.

You may even authorize another person, acting as your agent, to stake or locate a mining claim for you. However, the importance of doing everything correctly ordinarily makes it risky if you do not either do the job yourself or at least closely supervise it.

SELLING AND BUYING

A valid mining claim may be sold or bought, willed or inherited. However, if you sell or buy a claim, you acquire only such rights as are possessed under the mining law. If the claim is without a valid discovery or is otherwise defective, it is not made valuable by being sold or purchased.

A great deal of unwise speculation has resulted from the activities of unethical or, at the least, misinformed promoters who for a fee purport to stake mining claims and do annual assessment work for others. Most of these claims have been located in areas of rapid expansion and quickly changing land values. More often than not, such claims have absolutely no value for minerals and are invalid.

Such promoters are not a part of the mining industry and should not be confused with legitimate miners and prospectors diligently looking for minerals and who, on occasion, wish to sell a valid claim to others for development. Through the inducement of unethical promoters who misrepresent a mining claim as a possible site for a weekend cabin or hunting camp, numerous people have invested their money in worthless claims and have sometimes built a house only to discover that their supposed title to the land was not valid. In any event, an unpatented mining claim is to be used for mining purposes solely.

You may build a cabin or other improvements such as tool sheds and ore storage bins, etc. on a valid mining claim when such a structure is reasonably necessary for your use in connection with your mining operations.

BUREAU OF LAND MANAGEMENT LAND OFFICES

Alaska
SOUTHERN ALASKA
> Anchorage Land Office
> 555 Cordova Street
> Anchorage, Alaska 99501

NORTHERN ALASKA
> Fairbanks District & Land Office
> 516 Second Avenue
> Fairbanks, Alaska 99701

California
NORTHERN CALIFORNIA
> Sacramento Land Office
> Federal Building
> Room 4017
> Sacramento, California 95814

SOUTHERN CALIFORNIA
> Riverside District & Land Office
> 1414 Eight Street
> Riverside, California 92502

Colorado
> Colorado Land Office, Federal Building
> 1961 Stout Street
> Denver, Colorado 80202

Eastern
ARKANSAS, IOWA, LOUISIANA, MISSOURI, MINNESOTA (minerals only), and all STATES EAST OF THE MISSISSIPPI RIVER.
> Eastern States Land Office
> 7981 Eastern Avenue
> Silver Spring, Maryland 20910

Idaho
> Idaho Land Office, Federal Building
> Boise, Idaho 83701

Montana
MONTANA, NORTH DAKOTA, and SOUTH DAKOTA
> Montana Land Office
> 316 North 26th Street
> Billings, Montana 59101

Nevada
> Nevada Land Office, Federal Building &
> U.S. Nevada Courthouse
> 300 Booth Street
> Reno, Nevada 89502

New Mexico
NEW MEXICO, OKLAHOMA, and TEXAS
> New Mexico Land Office,
> Federal Building & U.S. Post Office
> South Federal Place
> Santa Fe, New Mexico 87501

Oregon
OREGON and WASHINGTON
> Oregon Land Office
> 729 Northeast Oregon Street
> Portland, Oregon 97232

Utah
> Utah Land Office, Federal Building
> Salt Lake City, Utah 84111

Wyoming
WYOMING, KANSAS, and NEBRASKA
> Wyoming Land Office,
> U.S. Post Office & Courthouse
> 2120 Capital Avenue
> Cheyenne, Wyoming 82001

STAKING A CLAIM ON FEDERAL LANDS

REGIONAL OFFICES OF THE FOREST SERVICE

Alaska Region
Post Office Box 1628
Juneau, Alaska 99801

California Region
630 Sansome Street
San Francisco, California 94111

Intermountain Region
324 25th Street
Ogden, Utah 84401

Northern Region
Federal Building
Missoula, Montana 59801

Pacific Northwest Region
Post Office Box 3623
Portland, Oregon 97208

Rocky Mountain Region
Federal Center, Building 85
Denver, Colorado 80225

Southern Region
Suite 800
1720 Peachtree Rd. N.W.
Atlanta, Georgia 30309

Southwestern Region
517 Gold Avenue S.W.
Albuquerque, New Mexico 87101

Chapter Twelve

GETTING A DEED TO YOUR CLAIM

A PATENTED MINING claim is a piece of ground for which the Federal Government has given a deed or passed its title to an individual. An unpatented claim, then, is one on which an individual, by the act of valid location under the mining laws, has obtained a right to extract and remove minerals from the ground but where full title has not been acquired from the U.S. Government. The rights under each claim are somewhat different.

You may apply for a patent to a mining claim if you wish, but it is not necessary to have a patent to mine and remove minerals from a valid claim.

If you establish a legal claim, perform and record annual assessment work required by state law, and meet all other requirements of Federal and state mining laws and regulations, you set up a possessory right to the area covered by the claim for the purpose of developing and extracting minerals. This possessory right may be sold or willed according to state law. Without your consent, no one else may mine the minerals you have claimed.

However, until you obtain patent to the claim from the Government, you do not hold full title to the land. Your possession is based upon discovery of a valuable mineral, and your right to the claim may be questioned or challenged by the Government if it appears your claim lacks discovery, the minerals have been mined out, or the claim does not meet other requirements of the law. If the Government's assertion is successful, the claim is cancelled and you have no more rights to the land.

On unpatented claims, you may use as much of the surface and the surface resources of the claim as are necessary for carrying on your mining operations. These uses, however, must be connected with and necessary for mineral development. A mining patent or deed received from the Government not only gives you exclusive right to the locatable minerals, but in most instances you also receive full title to the land surface and all other resources.

PRELIMINARY STEPS

The patenting of a mining claim may be somewhat expensive, particularly if a lode claim is involved. Claimants should fully inform themselves regarding the legal requirements that must be satisfied before a patent may be issued. The most essential requirement is that there be a discovery of a valuable mineral deposit within the boundaries of each claim.

Although the mining statutes do not specifically define a valuable mineral deposit, the courts have held that a valid discovery has been made when minerals have been found and the evidence is of such a character that an individual of ordinary prudence would be justified in the further expenditure of labor and means, with a reasonable prospect of developing a valuable mine. Profitability, based on present-day economics, is an important consideration in applying the prudent-man rule.

Many have misunderstood the test to mean that merely any showing of a mineral, or a hope or wish for future discovery, is enough. This is incorrect according to recent practices. There must be an actual physical discovery of the mineral on each mining claim, and the amount present must satisfy the prudent-man rule. Without a qualifying discovery, not only will the patent application be rejected, but action must ensue through appropriate administrative proceedings to cancel the entire claim.

With a few exceptions, all valuable mineral deposits on public domain lands belonging to the United States are open to prospecting, location, and purchase under the mining laws of 10 May 1872, as amended. The exceptions include:

1. Mineral deposits on the Outer Continental Shelf.

2. Deposits of common varieties of mineral materials such as gravel, sand, pumice, clay, stone, cinders, and such.

3. Minerals in lands which are disposable only under special provisions of law.

4. Those minerals commonly referred to as Leasing Act Minerals such as oil, gas, coal, potash, sodium, phosphate, oil shale, bitumen, asphalt, bituminous rock or sand, and, in Louisiana and New Mexico, sulphur.

Only U.S. citizens or those who have declared their intention to become citizens may occupy and purchase lands on which mineral deposits are located. Although our immigration laws no longer require a declaration of intent as a part of the naturalization procedure, one may still make such a declaration for the purpose of satisfying other laws.

The locator or owner of a valid mining location has the right to its exclusive possession for mining purposes and is not required to file for patent. He may hold the land for mining purposes so long as he performs labor or makes improvements thereon, or for the benefit of, worth no less than $100 each assessment year and so long as the land continues to be valuable for locatable minerals. The assessment year begins on 1 September following the date of location and ends on the same day the following year.

Upon failure to comply with the assessment work requirement, the claim is open to relocation by others. Thus, while a mining claim may be held and mined under the location title, that title may be lost by failure to perform the required annual assessment work. Once a final certificate for the claim is issued, though, annual assessment work is no longer necessary.

Before a patent may be obtained, not less than $500 must have been expended in labor and/or improvements in the development of the claim. This work may be done any time before applying for a patent.

SURVEYS

A mining claimant who wishes to patent a lode or placer claim on unsurveyed ground, or a claim described by metes and bounds such as a gulch placer, must have his claim surveyed. This survey must be done under the authority of the cadastral engineer (one specifically concerned with the extent, value, and ownership of pieces of land) of the Bureau of Land Management land district where the claim is located. This also applies to applications for mill sites, except mill sites located in conjunction with placer claims conforming to a legal subdivision.

An application form for survey may be obtained from the Bureau of Land Management cadastral engineer who will also provide a list of U.S. mineral surveyors. The applicant must choose his surveyor from this list and enter into a private agreement with him. The United States makes no warranty as to the quality of the work performed.

A deposit is required to cover the cost of making plats and field notes for each claim, each noncontiguous claim requiring a separate survey and deposit.

POSTING ON CLAIM

Where a survey is required, the patent applicant will post a copy of the plat and a notice of intention to apply for patent before making application. Where a survey is not required, only a notice of intention to apply for patent need be posted.

The papers posted should be protected from the elements, yet be in a conspicuous place on the claim or on one of the group of claims. These papers must remain posted during the 60-day publication period, the claimant being required to make a sworn statement that the notice and plat were continuously posted during this period.

APPLICATION FOR PATENT

Each application for patent must be filed in duplicate and be accompanied by a non-refundable $25 filing fee.

The application must show right of possession to the claim and state briefly, but clearly, the facts constituting the basis of his right to patent. This means that you must show discovery of a valuable mineral deposit within the limits of the claim there located and also that not less than $500 has been expended for the development of the claims (all work may be performed on just one of the claims as long as the other claims are benefited by this work).

You must state whether you have had any direct or indirect part in the development of the atomic energy program.

The application and all supporting statements must be signed within the land district where the claim is located. Individual claimants must all sign the application. If a claimant is absent, then the application must be signed by an attorney-in-fact within the land district. An attorney for an individual must have an original or certified copy of Power of Attorney.

An application by a corporation may be signed by its officers or by an agent or duly authorized attorney. A corporation attorney is attested by a certified copy of a resolution appointing or authorizing the proper official to appoint him, along with the original copy of Power of Attorney in the latter case.

LODE AND PLACER TERMS

A patent application for a lode or placer claim must describe fully the reasons why the deposit claimed is believed to be a valuable mineral deposit. As appropriate, this application would cover data, discussions, and analysis covering such items as general geology, results of drilling, sampling, nature of mineralization, likely mining method, estimated mining and milling costs, beneficiation or metallurgical processes, transportation factors, market data and analysis, sales prices, expenses, etc.

If you are applying for a patent to a lode claim, you will be required to furnish a full description of the vein or lode, and state whether ore has been extracted and if so the amount and value. You must also describe where, within the limits of the claim, the vein or lode is exposed. In addition to improvements mentioned in the field notes, you will be obliged to describe in detail: shafts, cuts, tunnels, or other workings claimed as improvements, giving dimensions, value, course, and distance to the nearest survey corner.

If you are applying for a patent to a placer claim, you must show that the land applied for is placer ground containing valuable mineral deposits not in vein or lode formation, plus the fact that you are seeking title because of the mineral therein and not to control water courses or to obtain valuable timber. The statement must relate to the character of the deposit and the natural features of the ground. The following details should be covered as fully as possible.

1. If the claim is for a deposit of placer gold, give the yield per cubic yard as shown by prospecting and development work, the thickness of any gold-bearing gravels, thickness of overburden, formation and extent of deposit, and all other data indicating that the claim is valuable because of its deposits of placer gold.

2. Of course, you may come across some other metal such as platinum or silver while prospecting for gold. If the claim involves a deposit other than gold, you must fully describe the amount, nature, and extent of the deposits, plus any additional reasons you regard it as a

valuable mineral claim. The natural features of the claim must be described completely. For instance, give an account of streams as to their course, amount of water carried, and fall within the claim. State the kind and amount of timber and other vegetation and their adapatability to mining and other uses.

3. If the placer claim is all placer ground, that must be both stated in the application and also supported by statements of proof. If the claim is mixed placer and lode, this should be set forth, along with the description of all known veins situated within the boundaries of the placer claim. A specific declaration must be furnished for each lode intended to be claimed. Whether the lode is claimed or excluded, it must be surveyed and marked on the plat. The field notes and plat must give separately the area of the lode veins and the area of the placer ground. All other known lodes are, by the silence of the applicant, excluded by law from all claim by him, of whatever nature, possessory or otherwise.

4. Inasmuch as no examination and report by a mineral surveyor is available in cases of claims taken by legal subdivisions, you should describe in detail all shafts, cuts, tunnels, and other workings claimed as improvements, as well as the dimensions, value, course, and distance to the nearest corner of the public surveys. All such statements of proof must be in duplicate.

MILL SITE CLAIMS

Lands entered as mill sites, each not exceeding five acres of nonmineral land, may be included in a patent application for a lode or placer mining claim and may be patented with one of them. The mill sites may also be patented in separate procedures.

In conjunction with mill claims, the mill site must be noncontiguous to the vein or lode. But it has been held that a mill site in conjunction with a lode claim may touch a side line, provided the claimant demonstrates that the lode or vein does not extend into any part of the ground covered by the mill site. Such a mill site must be used or occupied for mining or milling purposes in conjunction with a valid mining claim.

The owner of a quartz mill or reduction works, who does not own a mine in conjunction with one of these, may still locate and receive a patent for a mill site.

Where nonmineral land is needed, used, and occupied by the holder of a valid placer mining claim for mining, milling, beneficiation, processing, or other operations in connection with his claim, the mill site may be included in his mining claim patent application.

Mill sites located in conjunction with lode claims and independent mill sites must be surveyed and the purchase money paid at the same rate applicable to lode claims, that is, $5 an acre or any fraction of an acre. Mill sites located in connection with placer claims and taken by legal subdivisions need no further survey. They may be patented upon payment of the purchase price of $2.50 an acre or any fraction of an acre.

The procedure of securing a patent for a mill site is the same as that for getting a patent to a lode or placer claim. When included in an application for a lode claim, a copy of the application and one of the plat must be posted on the mill site as well as on the lode claim. Where an application is filed for an independent mill site, a copy of the notice must be posted on the claim. A notice of intention to apply for a patent must be posted on a mill site located in connection with a placer claim.

All applications to patent mill sites must be accompanied by statements of proof by two or more disinterested persons as to the non-mineral character of the land. Use or occupation of the land for mill site purposes must be shown. In the case of an independent mill site, proof of the improvements and use of these must be shown.

SUPPORTING PAPERS FOR PATENT APPLICATION

The patent application, for which no form has been established, must be filed in the land office after notice of application for patent, together with a copy of the plat if a mineral survey has been made and has been posted on the claim. It must be supported by:

1. *Two copies apiece of the field notices and the survey.*

2. *Proof of posting on claim.* Statements of two credible witnesses, not the claimants or their attorneys in fact, giving the date and place of posting, with a copy of the notice being attached to these statements.

3. *Evidence of title.* Each patent application must be supported by either a certificate of title or a certified abstract of title for each claim. Each certificate must be accompanied by single certified copies of the original and amended location notices of each claim.

The certificate of title or the abstract must be current to a day reasonably near the date the application is filed. It must be executed by a state-authorized abstractor or title company and in a form that is satisfactory to the Director of the Bureau of Land Management.

The applicant, as soon as practicable, must file a supplemental certificate or abstract current to the date of filing or application.

The applicant, as evidence of his ownership of the claim, may furnish, instead of a certificate or abstract of title, a certified copy of the statute of limitations applicable to mining claims in the state. In addition, the applicant must furnish a statement including the following facts:

a. Origin and maintenance of his title.

b. Area of claim.

c. Amount and extent of mining improvements.

d. Whether his title has been disputed in court proceedings or otherwise, explaining in detail any such disputes.

e. Other matters known to him which bear upon his right of possession.

The above statement should be supported by statements of any disinterested individuals knowledgeable of the facts relative to the applicant's location, occupancy, possession, improvements, etc.

The applicant must also file a certificate, under the seal of the court having jurisdiction, that no suit or action involving right of possession to the claim is pending. This certificate should also state that there has been no litigation in the court affecting title to the claim for the time fixed by the state's statute of limitations other than that which has been decided in favor of the patent applicant.

4. *Proof of citizenship.* Statements of citizenship may be signed either within or without the land district by:

a. A native-born citizen, who must state that fact, giving the date and place of his birth.

b. A person who has declared his intention to become a citizen or who has been naturalized. He must have a statement showing date, place, and the court before which he declared his intention or from which his naturalization papers came, plus the certificate number if known.

c. An association that must furnish competent evidence relative to a. and b. above, regarding each of its members.

d. A corporation that must furnish a certified copy of its charter or certificate of incorporation.

5. *Payment of filing fee.*

6. *Publisher's agreement.* The land office manager will designate the newspaper in which the publication will appear.

7. *Notice for publication.* The notice of application must be published at the applicant's expense either in 9 consecutive insertions in a weekly paper or in 9 consecutive Wednesday insertions in a daily

paper. A sample form containing essential data is contained in Title 43, Code of Federal Regulations.

8. *Notice for posting in land office.*

FINAL PROCEDURES

The applicant must furnish the following before the issuance of the Final Certificate of Mineral Entry:

1. *Proof of publication.* The sworn statement of the publisher that the notice was published for the statutory period, noting the first and last date of publication.

2. *Statement of posting.* Statement showing that the mineral survey plat and notice of application for the patent remained conspicuously posted upon the subject claim during the 60-day publication period. The dates of posting must be given.

3. *Statement of charges and fees paid by him.*

4. *Payment of purchase price.* The purchase price shall be as follows:

   a. Lode claim and/or mill site in connection with it: $5 for each acre and fractional part of an acre.

   b. Placer claim and/or mill site in connection with it: $2.50 for each acre and fractional part of an acre.

   c. Mill site for quartz mill where applicant does not own a lode claim: $5 for each acre and fractional part of an acre.

ADVERSE CLAIMS

Any adverse claims must be filed within the 60-day period of publication by the adverse claimant or his attorney-in-fact, with proof of authority, within the land district. They must set forth the nature and extent of the conflict and the interest of the adverse claimant, with a certified copy of the adverse claim location certificate. Unless the claim is described by legal subdivisions, a plat showing the extent and boundaries of the adverse claim and the conflict should be filed.

Suit must be commenced in a court of competent jurisdiction to determine the right of possession within 30 days from the date of filing of the adverse claim, and it must be diligently prosecuted to final judgment.

Upon the filing of an adverse claim and commencement of suit, all proceedings in the Land Office will be suspended until the controversy is settled or the adverse claim waived.

A copy of the judgment roll certified by the Clerk of Court, or his certificate that the suit has been dismissed or withdrawn, is required as proof of termination of suit.

LAND OFFICE PROCEDURES

Although the routine in processing may vary from case to case, the following is a very general outline of the steps taken in the Land Office, necessary and incidental to processing a mineral patent application.

Upon receipt, a patent application will be scanned for sufficiency and conformity with statute and regulations. If it is found to be incomplete, the applicant will be so advised and ordinarily allowed a reasonable time in which to correct the deficiency.

The status of the land will be investigated by the Land Office. If all is in order, the record will be forwarded to the Office of the Solicitor for a title opinion. Unless full possessory title is vested in the patent applicant, in most instances further processing will be suspended until such time as the full title is demonstrated. A patent may not issue unless full possessory rights are vested in the applicant.

When the application, including proof of full possessory title, is complete and all else is regular, the Land Office Manager will check the proposed publication for accuracy. He will furnish the applicant with the name of the newspaper in which the Notice of Applicant is to be published. The applicant will be required to furnish the agreement of the publisher to hold the applicant alone responsible for the cost of the publication.

A copy of the notice of application will be posted in the Land Office for the full period of publication. A copy of the first publication must be furnished the Land Office where it will again be checked for accuracy. If any correction is needed, the publisher will be so advised, following which the correct notice must be published for the full period required as though the first publication had not been made. If the fault is the publisher's, he will bear any additional costs. The Government will handle the additional charge if the error is the fault of the Land Office.

Upon receipt and approval of Proofs of Publication and Posting, the record will once more be checked for completeness. All proper fees and costs must be paid by the applicant, and the publisher's statement that the publication is complete must be filed. The statement of the applicant showing the notice of the application was posted on the claim during the entire 60-day period must be furnished. Then, in the absence of any adverse claim, the purchase price having been paid, Final Certificate of Mineral Entry will be issued.

The issuance of final certificate does not mean that the patent proceedings are ended, however. Prior to the issuance of the patent, validity of the mining claim must be verified. But no assessment work need be performed after the issuance of a final certificate.

The case record will be referred to a Government mineral examiner for verification that a valuable mineral deposit has been discovered, that the improvements necessary for patent have been made, and that the other legal requirements have been met. Where the land covered by the patent application is within a National Forest, the claim will be examined by a mineral examiner of the U.S. Forest Service. Elsewhere, the claim will be examined by a Bureau of Land Management mineral examiner. Such employees are professional geologists, geological engineers, or mining engineers.

The Government mineral examiners will normally advise the mining claimant of the date set for an examination of a mining claim and invite him to accompany them in their examination. Where possible, the examination will be scheduled to accommodate the applicant. Discovery points must be available for inspection. Examiners are not expected to make a discovery for the mining claimant, to renovate discovery points, or to make examinations where workings are unsafe.

The Government mining examiner is expected to be completely impartial. His examination, ideally, will be objective and in accordance with accepted professional and industry practices. He is not authorized to offer his opinion at the time nor to discuss the merits of the claim.

If all is in order, a discovery demonstrated and other requirements met, the claim will be cleared for patenting. However, if a discovery is not verified, the Government may initiate a contest proceeding against the claim.

A contest is an inquiry into the validity of a mining claim. The mining claimant is advised of the inquiry by the service of a complaint. If he denies allegations contained in the complaint and does this within the time provided, a hearing will be held in accordance with the Administrative Procedure Act.

At this hearing he will be afforded opportunity to cross-examine the Government's witness and to offer evidence, including expert testimony, to substantiate his assertion of the validity of the claim. The hearing is presided over by a Hearing Examiner who will render a decision only after full consideration of the law and all evidence submitted by the parties. Adverse decisions are subject to appeal.

Although in certain instances the patent will convey only a limited title or a title with certain restrictions, ordinarily a mining claim or mill site patent will convey the whole of the Government's title to the land covered by the claim. Such a conveyance in fee simple transfers the property to private ownership. The mining claimant may thereafter use the land as any other private property. The land will, of course, be subject to taxes and local ordinances.

Chapter Thirteen

PROSPECTING KIT

YOU'LL WANT AT least a small gold pan which can be made of aluminum if you're doing much backpacking. A compact, folding shovel of the armed forces type may be picked up at a surplus store. You'll need a light, inexpensive cloth tape measuring 50 to 100 feet for laying out your claim. A small, 10-power, folding pocket magnifying glass will be sufficient for examining specimens.

Bring along some small, drawstring cloth sacks to use as sample bags. You'll want a horseshoe or bar magnet for separating magnetic minerals from your gold. If there's lode gold in your region, take along a prospector's pick. Location notices, to be completed on the spot, are available at stationery and general stores in mining country.

There are, of course, other items that may be useful depending upon how lightly you are traveling; for instance, a steel or iron mortar and pestle for grinding samples for panning. Or you can use an ordinary two-inch pipe cap and your prospector's pick. For placer work, you may also want a sieve or screen with 60 to 80 holes per square inch for limiting the material you pan.

MATCHES

The handiest and most durable matches in the field are the long, wooden, strike-anywhere, kitchen variety. For extended trips, it's sound procedure to waterproof a large container of such matches with melted paraffin, thus always assuring yourself of a supply.

The best way to carry an emergency supply of these matches on your person is in an unbreakable waterproof container that can be fastened to the clothing. The neat, little, cylindrical, metal cases that have been manufactured for years by the Marble Arms Corporation, Gladstone, Michigan 49837 and which sell for about a dollar are the best I've ever seen. I carry two of these whenever in primitive wilderness, keeping safely one to a pocket the few extra matches I'll ordinarily be using during the day.

METAL MATCH

One of the most important inventions of recent years for outdoorsmen everywhere is the Metal Match, invented by William Sampson and manufactured and distributed by the Ute Mountain Corporation of Englewood, Colorado 80110. It is made of eleven different rare earth metals, extruded from inert gas under extremely high pressures. The result is a waterproof, fireproof, non-toxic, and durably stubby gray stick which will light from 1,000 to 3,000 fires, depending on its size.

This Metal Match is fast and simple to use. You shave small bits from it with the back of your knife, a sharp rock, bit of broken glass, or any other hard sharp object. These pieces are bunched in a small area, among tinder such as birch bark or an abandoned dry nest if you're lighting a campfire, then ignited with a spark from the Match. This is produced with a rapid downward stroke with the same sharp hard substance.

The spark carries heat of 2,800° F., but due to the short time it lasts it is safe even in inexperienced hands. It can also be used to light stoves, barbeques, grills, and so on, and is the next best thing to a regular match. One will really round out a camping kit from the simplest to the most elaborate.

COMPASS

The compass can be used at any time nearly everywhere to keep you informed on how to get back, whereas bad weather can make celestial determinations impossible for days at a stretch. You'll need

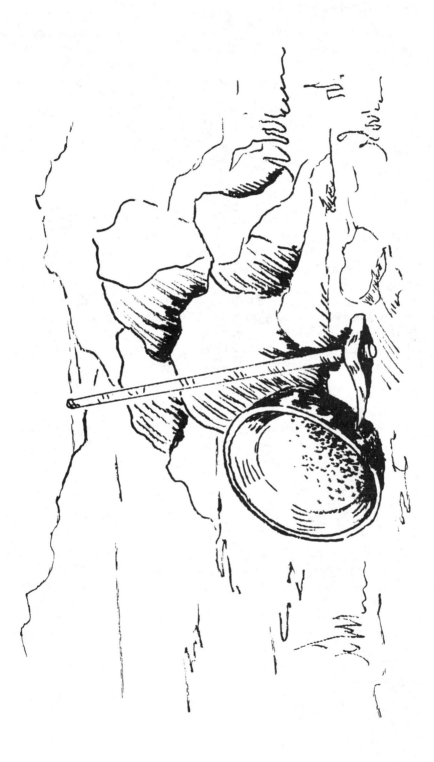

one, also, to lay out your claim. You should have at least one compass with you whenever in even familiar wilderness. In wild country I also like to carry a spare Williams Guide Line pin-on compass fastened to my shirt, just in case. The philosophy of hoping for the best but preparing for the worst is not a bad one—back of beyond.

Compasses are inexpensive, and they can be compact. You should have a rugged, accurate, waterproof, durable, lightweight, and luminous instrument such as the above on which to rely.

WATCH

A substantial and reasonably accurate watch, not necessarily an expensive one by any means, comes close to being a modern-day necessity, especially as for everyday traveling in the Farther Places where distances are measured less often by miles than by the time it takes to traverse them.

With this watch, too, you can accurately determine direction as explained in such a camping book as my *Skills For Taming The Wilds*. Suppose you forget to wind it one day. Then set it precisely by the sun, as detailed in the same volume.

GLASSES

If you need prescription lenses to get around with, you'll find it only prudent to carry a second pair in a substantial protective case. You'll also be wise to bring along a pair of optically correct, stanchly made sunglasses if you expect to find yourself in desert, snow, or high country.

ADHESIVE BANDAGES

It's always a good idea to have with you a few of these little gauze pads, each centered on a short strip of adhesive tape. Application of one promptly to a part of the foot that is becoming tender will many times prevent otherwise crippling blisters. Too, one is often useful for repairs. These bandages are best carried in the sterile coverings in which the better of them are sold, particularly as the wrappings have the additional value of preserving the maximum adhesive power.

Plain white gauze is medically superior to treated pads for general use, although you may well prefer a non-stick brand. Plastic tape will adhere and fit better than fabric. When used on potential or actual blisters, the dry adhesive bandage can safely be left in place until the skin toughens, as it permits healing air to reach the affected part.

KNIFE

A knife comes close to being a necessity for carrying on your person or in the kit. As always there is a best for the purpose. This in my opinion is the Bradford Angier Survival Knife, made on order and by hand by W. D. Randall, Jr., P.O. Box 1988, Orlando, Florida 32802. Despite the name, I have no financial interest whatsoever with Mr. Randall or his knife, so I feel free to recommend it unreservedly.

This is the sort of lastingly sharp, intrinsically rugged sheath knife you can use for everything from butchering to cutting corner stakes or building a shelter. It comes in a substantial leather case with a handy carborundum sharpening stone in a separate compartment on its front.

A functional compass is embedded in the durable Micarta handle which is a strongly laminated phenolic composed of hundreds of layers of linen, impregnated with phenolic and cured under high pressure and heat.

AX

Both the light belt ax and the more substantial hatchet can be useful, but for more practical prospecting use you may well select a good Hudson Bay ax with its cut-away butt that saves weight and its regular-size cutting surface. Such axes are obtainable with ruggedly riveted leather sheaths. If such a covering is not included, wrap the blade safely as with canvas before entrusting it to your outfit.

SAW

There are a number of folding saws on the market, but those I have tested have been awkward and fragile, not for the hard use you'd need to put them to when caught out in cold weather. Instead, for a long-haul kit, I'd recommend the inclusion of a Swede saw blade. This ribbon of narrow thin steel weighs little, and it can be rolled into a plate-wide bundle and safely encased in canvas.

One of the two-piece tubular-steel handles adds up to little extra weight and not a great deal of bulk. Then when everything is assembled you have an efficient tool. On the other hand, you can bring the blade by itself, plus a pair of butterfly bolts, and bend a stout green sapling into use for your handle.

GUNS AND AMMO

A light, scope-sighted, accurate big game repeating rifle, such as a Winchester Model 70 .30-06, is the most valuable weapon you can have with you for living to a certain extent off a big-game region. If you were in the Central American jungles, on the other hand, the most functional caliber for the small game there would be more like a .22 Hornet.

Cartridges should be picked for their meat-anchoring efficiency. If two or three firearms are to be brought by a party, all ideally should be alike so that the parts of any can be drafted to keep at least one operative.

PLASTIC

Two pieces of light plastic sheeting, each six feet square, can secure up to three quarts of water a day for you even in the driest desert. The simple and successful operation of such a solar still is detailed in my *Skills For Taming The Wilds*. You could carry both these plastic squares folded in a breast pocket, and they'd have innumerable other uses.

The hardest part of building any brush shelter lies in waterproofing the roof, and the sandwiching of an area of light plastic in this area of perhaps evergreen boughs will assure dryness. Too, the plastic alone can be quickly turned into rainy-day shelters for as long as you're outdoors. There are innumerable other uses, such as bringing game liver or fish cleanly back to camp, etc.

A sheet of plastic, eight feet long by four feet wide, is what I've carried in the North Woods for years, in a shirt pocket where it occupies no more space than a handkerchief. Although I've used it innumerable times, it's interesting to note that I've not yet had to replace it.

TENT OR TARP

A small, tough, flyproof, lightweight tent will be preferable to a tarpaulin only when you are near civilization, where there are insects to be excluded, when the time and energy available for erecting a shelter is limited, and where it is difficult to pitch and maintain a fabric shelter as on a mountaintop.

Otherwise, a small tarp will prove more adaptable, pleasant, and efficient as at least part of a lean-to, open to a companionable fire. It can even be used in bad fly country with the addition of an individual mosquito bar apiece.

SLEEPING BAG

White goose down in its prime grades is the lightest and warmest insulation securable for the making of sleeping bags. The darker goose down is almost as good. Duck down is not quite as effective, although some manufacturers work this less expensive filler into their top garments and advertise the whole as waterfowl down.

Cheap sleeping bags may have the bulkier, colder, and much less expensive feathers of the fowl mixed in with the down. You're apt to get what you pay for. A well-constructed sleeping bag with one of the man-made fibers such as dacron is preferable to a shoddy feather bag.

The best fabric in which to enclose the filler is at this writing light, tough nylon. Its slipperiness makes it less constricting and easier to get into. Although initially cold to the touch, it warms swiftly and actually absorbs less heat than does, for instance, cotton flannel which feels warm the moment you come in contact with it.

If you have the use for a sleeping bag, it will be shortsighted to try to save too much money in this department except on junior bags which will be soon outgrown. Shop warily. The best bags on the market are those sold and sometimes made by the large, catalog-issuing outdoor equipment outfitters. Study the catalog of several before you decide on your purchase.

If you have a choice, snaps are far less vulnerable than even the stoutest zipper. Most functional, too, is a robe that will open flat.

You'll want either an air or one of the newer foam mattresses to go under your bag. For air mattresses, it may be useful to note that I am still using my original rubber, bulblike pump that works with either hands or feet. For those who need a pillow, one of the small affairs that inflates in a few seconds by mouth is convenient. Again, conscientiously manufactured models of any of the above will last for years.

MEDICINE KIT

Unreservedly recommended is the four-ounce medicine kit described in detail in *Being Your Own Wilderness Doctor* by E.

Russel Kodet, M.D., and myself, which can be used to treat everything from a cut to dysentery. Such a kit might well save you and your companion's life under wilderness conditions when no doctor is closer than days away.

SNAKEBITE KIT

If you are prospecting in poisonous-snake country, you'll be wise to carry at least one Cutter Snakebite Kit, inexpensively obtainable in any drugstore. Each of these contains three suction cups, a lymph constrictor, surgical scapel, and antiseptic, plus swiftly and simply understood illustrated instructions. Incidentally, most of the venomous snakebites in the United States are by rattlesnakes.

The suction cups in these neat and compact kits, each no larger than a 12-gauge shotgun shell, can also be used for bee stings and severe insect bites which may be treated by applying suction to the affected part without any cuts. But their main application is for snakebite.

This Cutter Kit was designed by Robert K. Cutter, M.D., after he'd encountered four rattlers in one day's fishing while the snakebite kit in his camping outfit was back in camp because it had proved too clumsy to carry. Most physicians today feel that first aid during the first half hour after a poisonous bite is extremely important and should be carried out by the one bitten or by the most competent individual at hand.

The new Cutter Snake Kit, dramatically improved by the same Bob Cutter, is now on the market. One of its features is that the new oval suction cups cover at one time two fang marks considerably farther apart than did the former round model. Perhaps even more important, the oval shape allows for gentle suction on soft skin by pressing the *Lo* side and stronger suction for tough hides by pressing the *Hi* side. Even the smallest Cub Scout will have plenty of strength in his fingers to press the *Lo* side. Some of them didn't, with the round ones.

Another thing, the three new suction cups are made of plastic rather than rubber and should hold their elasticity much longer, particularly if kept in a warm place. And the new lymph constrictor can be tightened or loosened with one hand, somewhat helpful when the bite is on the other hand or arm. The whole outfit, finally, is shorter and slimmer than the old one, hence more comfortable and more likely to be carried in the pocket.

CORD OR ROPE

A coil of good new rope, perhaps ⅜-inch manila, may be useful in a lot of different ways if you can manage the extra weight and bulk. If not, include at least a few yards of nylon cord, stout enough to hold your weight in an emergency.

SOAP

The best initial way to handle a cut or scrape, especially in the wilderness where help is not at hand, is to wash it with plenty of soap and water, then dry it well. Inasmuch as no soap is contained in the tiny four-ounce medicine kit which I recommended a few paragraphs back, a small bar should be packed elsewhere in the outfit.

You'll need it, too, to keep healthfully clean. Greasy dishes, on the other hand, will manufacture their own cleansing agent if boiled with water and wood ashes, the lye in the latter combining with the fats to make a soap. Then scour them if necessary with sand, moss, grass, or with the well-known rush known as horsetail which, when very young, also happens to be edible. When older, it becomes poisonous to eat.

There is now a sort of super soap called Trak that can be ordered in a light, handy tube from Freeman Industries, Inc., 100 Marbledale Road, Tuckahoe, New York 10707. With this concentrated foaming agent for outdoorsmen you can wash, shave, bathe, shampoo, cleanse clothes, or do the dishes better than with the bulkier essentials it replaces. Trak lathers speedily in cold, hard, or even salt water, and so little is needed to do the job that I find a tube lasts me a month even when used daily. For anyone who must travel light, it is another of the woodsman's modern-day boons.

TOILET KIT

This may be where you'll choose to carry your soap if the supply is to be limited. You'll also want a small rough towel that can be regularly washed, toothbrush, dentifrice which may be baking soda or table salt which will have utility elsewhere, comb, and any small items you may wish such as manicure scissors and safety razor with spare blades.

FLASHLIGHT

Despite the fact that there are several methods of making wilderness torches, a flashlight is considered pretty much of a necessity today when one is away from power. A conventional two-cell light is usually enough, preferably a model with smoothly rounded edges that will not be as likely to wear holes in a pocket.

An extra bulb, padded in cotton batten, can frequently be carried inside the spring at the end. I've always found it sound practice, also, to keep an additional spare elsewhere in the outfit. If you've the room for them, a couple of extra, long-lived batteries are also a good idea.

No matter what, the batteries will last markedly longer if you get in the habit of switching on the beam only for extremely short periods of time; all that will be necessary, for instance, when you're traveling through the woods at night. To preclude the accidental waste of power, use some stratagem such as reversing the batteries, putting paper between battery post and bulb, or taping the switch when the flashlight is packed.

INSECT REPELLENT

Mosquitoes, gnats, biting flies, and other such winged pests become so thick in some regions at certain times of the year that they can kill you. You should, by all means, have an effective insect repellent in your kit.

After prolonged personal experiments with different fly dopes in various parts of the continent, I can give unqualified recommendation to the new Cutter Insect Repellent, developed after years of research by Robert K. Cutter, M.D., and manufactured by Cutter Laboratories in Berkeley, California 94710. It is widely available at drugstores, sporting goods stores, and general stores who can secure it for you if they do not stock it already.

Although this effective repellent—in the Far North, where the mosquitoes are particularly bad, I found it also a fine psychological aid, as it kept away the sing of the insects as well as their sting—is the most expensive per ounce, it is at the same time the least costly and longest lasting of any practical preparation of the sort I've yet found on the market. Three drops for hands and face is plenty, even in the most bug-congested areas. It comes in a small plastic bottle, easy to pack and apply.

Suppose one day you find yourself prospecting in insect-infested wilderness without any commercial repellent of any sort? Smoke will keep the pests away to some extent, although this treatment becomes hard on lungs and eyes. Plastering exposed portions with mud works. Better still, if you can manage it, is keeping to exposed and windy country, for example along the breezy and open shores of a river.

A paste of water and baking soda will help relieve the discomfort of a few bites. Rubbing the area with a sliced wild apple, found throughout much of the continent, used to be considered a reasonably efficient healing agent.

One of the wild garlics may also save you a lot of discomfort. Tests conducted at the University of California at Riverside revealed that mosquitoes don't like garlic, especially in close quarters. In fact, five species of them keeled over dead when sprayed with a 12 parts of garlic to a million solution.

Garlic-eating individuals in Louisiana and elsewhere have long known the efficacy of dabbing a little of their underarm sweat around their exposed necks, wrists, and ankles. Just eat some wild food varieties, determined from a book like my full-color *Field Guide To Edible Wild Plants,* which, incidentally, points up the flavors of a lot of other wild delicacies. The garlic will then exude through your sweat glands, doing its bit in keeping hungry female skeeters at bay.

Pennyroyal, whose square stems and tiny blue flowers resemble the other mints, was the standby of outdoorsmen over much of the southeast quarter of the country in the days before mass-manufactured repellents. The odor of this wild plant suggests the pharmacy rather than the confectionery, by the way. Just crush the leaves between the fingers and rub over the exposed skin. The bruised leaves can also be scattered over and around sleeping bags in infected country.

The black walnut, a resident of most of the entire eastern half of the country, will also deter the bugs' appetites. Pick the long compound leaves where they bow near the ground, as well as any of the other leaflets within easy reach, and rub them where the critters are not desired. Perhaps the iodinelike stain on your fingers, when you separate the husks from the delicious nuts, is a clue as to why the biting bugs do not favor the black walnut.

But these are emergency methods at best. The difference between them and a tiny bottle of Cutter Insect Repellent is the same as that between a cap pistol and a .30-06 rifle.

PAPER AND PEN

When you are traveling without maps in strange country anywhere, a map sketched as you proceed will help to keep you straight. It is so necessary to maintain close contact with your whereabouts when prospecting, in fact, that even with maps you'll want to work closely where you go. In other words, your outfit should include some substantial paper and a pencil or, better still, a new and dependable pen.

When you come across any promising samples that you want to have later assayed, number the sample as with a bit of adhesive tape and a pen and note the number on your map.

WATER PURIFICATION TABLETS

The small two-ounce bottles that each hold 100 halazone tablets take up no more room than a shotgun shell and provide good insurance against the contaminated drinking water that may be encountered anywhere, even far from the ravages of man.

Because these tiny pellets function by releasing purifying chlorine gas into the questionable water, they should be fresh. Renew your supply periodically, in other words, and buy them from a reputable drugstore rather than from a surplus concern. The bottle should be kept firmly closed in a dark, preferably dry place.

No purification of water by chemical means is as safe as boiling it for five minutes at sea level and an additional minute for each extra 1,000 feet in elevation, but a couple of little halazone tablets will normally make a quart of water pure enough for human consumption in a half hour. If the water is especially suspicious or if it is muddy, it will be a wise precaution to use four halazone tablets and to let them remain for an hour.

When you boil water, all parts of the container become hot and purify themselves. With chemical disinfectants, on the other hand, you have to take care to purify all contact points so that once the water is purified, it will not easily be reinfected. If you are using halazone with your canteen, for instance, replace the cap loosely and wait for five minutes while the tablets dissolve. Then shake the contents diligently, permitting some of the liquid to slosh over the top and lid of the container. Tighten the cap then and leave it that way for the desired time before using any of the water.

Chlorine-releasing compounds cannot be depended on in semi-tropical and tropical regions. And, incidentally, it's erroneous to assume that the presence of a strong alcoholic beverage will render water harmless. Water in these areas should either be boiled or treated with something such as iodine water purification tablets. It was my friend the late Colonel Townsend Whelen who brought these facts to my attention well before these methods were adopted as standard for the U.S. armed forces.

Containing the active ingredient tetraglycine hydroperiodide, these small tablets have proved effective against all common water-borne bacteria, as well as the cysts of endamoeba histolutica and the cercariae of schistosomiasis.

Manufactured as Globaline by WTS Pharmaceuticals, Division of Wallace and Tiernan, Inc., in Rochester, New York 14623, 50 water-purifying tablets are packaged in a glass bottle with a wax-seal cap. Any drugstore can secure these for you. Added to water, each tablet frees eight milligrams of iodine which acts as the purification factor. One tablet will purify one quart of clear water.

These tablets, too, must be kept dry. The bottle, therefore, should be immediately and tightly capped after being opened. Directions for use are:

a. Add one tablet to a quart of clear water in container with cap, two tablets if not clear,

b. replace cap loose and wait 5 minutes,

c. shake well, allowing a little water to leak out and disinfect the screw threads before tightening containing cap,

d. wait 10 minutes before using for any purpose and if the water is very cold, wait 20 minutes.

You can use tincture of iodine instead of iodine water purification tablets. Eight drops of reasonably fresh 2½% tincture of iodine, utilized like the above tablets, will purify a quart of water in 10 minutes. It will be a good idea to let it stand 20 minutes if the water, as it may be in the mountains, is extremely cold.

FISHING OUTFIT

This need not be elaborate. A few yards of good tough line, perhaps half a dozen hooks, and some of the small strips of lead that can be twisted into position as sinkers should catch enough fish for a change in diet from time to time. I keep such a tiny kit in my pocket whenever I'm in the bush. You're usually where you can cut a pole on the spot.

ASSEMBLED EMERGENCY KITS

There are a number of pre-assembled emergency kits on the market, and inasmuch as they take up little room, some may care to include one or more in their outfit for perhaps carrying in a pocket when away from camp in the wilderness. I've tested two such kits in the Far North and found them of substantial value for anyone temporarily delayed, injured, lost, or isolated by fire, flood, storm, or other mishap. Both are packed by Chuck Wagon Foods, Micro Drive, Woburn, Massachusetts 01801.

The Pocket-Size Emergency Food Kit, weighing eight ounces and fitting in a sport shirt pocket, has been dipped in wax so that it's waterproof and will actually float. Its total food value is 650 calories, and it's actually a panic preventer, meant to take care of situations when you may be unexpectedly out overnight and before you settle into any perhaps necessary long-term pull.

It contains a compressed cereal bar, starch jelly bar, two non-melting chocolate bars, a single-edge razor blade, two bandaids, toilet tissue, wax-dipped wooden matches, a hank of 12-pound-test monofilament line, three fishhooks, three salt packets, a heavy aluminum foil container, and a survival instruction booklet.

Chuck Wagon's Woodsman's Emergency Kit is about twice as large and holds 750 calories of food in the form of pemmican, tropical chocolate bars, and the like, as well as a fire starter, moistureproof matches, toilet tissue, water purification tablets, a plastic water bag, bandaids, razor blade, aluminum foil, and, perhaps most important, an emergency compass.

WALLE-HAWK

The single most ingenious and functional survival tool on the market is the Walle-Hawk, so called because it can be easily carried in a wallet 365 days a year and because it is as handy to the modern survivor as the tomahawk was to the primitive Indian. This was invented by Jessie Morrision and is manufactured and distributed by the Allison Forge Corp., Box 404, Belmont, Massachusetts 02178. The Walle-Hawk can do everything from digging edible roots to skinning game and signaling for help. Suspended by a thread, string, or hair, it is also an accurate compass. It will last a lifetime.

FOAM RUBBER PADDING

It is quite easy for even an experienced woodsman to bruise the tissue of the foot. This only requires striking the arch on a ridge or bending the foot in an unnatural way. An injury of this sort is very painful to walk on. If you are hiking, a bit of foam rubber may make all the difference. A sheet of ½-inch foam rubber padding about a foot square, obtainable from your drugstore or a surgical supply house, can be used to pad fragile articles in the kit, while a section can be easily cut off to fit inside a boot to pad and support the injured foot.

"I have found that the best method is to hold the pad against the bottom of the foot by placing it inside one's sock," Peter A. Crichton of Rochester, N.Y., biologist with the Rochester Institute of Technology, advises me. "This avoids the use of tape which can in itself be a discomfort. As for the size of the pad to use, this should be experimented with by the injured party. Generally a section several inches shorter by about half-inch narrower than the foot will relieve pressure on most bruises.

"I have walked on such a pad for up to four days," Mr. Crichton told me, "in moderately rough terrain in relative comfort on an injury which, without the pad, made walking extremely painful. Of course, healing such an injury requires rest, but when this is out of the question one can get along on such a pad."

REPAIR OUTFIT

You'll have your own needs and ideas for this. Mine, I find, has changed little over recent years after a lot of initial adding and discarding. I carry it in a little zippered ditty bag I secured from the catalog-issuing L. L. Bean, Freeport, Maine 04032 three decades ago.

The present contents include: a small, fine pair of pointed scissors, the best I could find. Small pointed tweezers, also the finest obtainable, valuable for minor repairs and for removing especially pesky slivers and thorns, as well as for picking up gold flakes. Two rolls of narrow fabric adhesive tape, valuable for mending as well as for personal uses, and for numbering samples, particularly if in cold weather it is warmed before applying. A roll of dental floss.

Pliers with a fine cutting edge—that could slice through the shank of a fishhook, for example, if someone in the party is ever unfortunate enough to get one in his body—and with tightly fitting edges that have removed porcupine quills from a dog. Incidentally, such quills pull out more easily if their tops are first cut off to ease the suction that helps hold their barbed points in place.

A nested set of screwdrivers with handles rugged enough to be held by the pliers. A bit of nylon fishline rolled on cardboard. Rawhide lacing. A coil of snare wire to keep me in meat if the need ever arises. Recently, I've also been carrying a small, compact, very light clasp knife with two excellent cutting blades, scissors, file, screwdriver, and can opener.

A small tube, well wrapped, of all-purpose adhesive. A small file for sharpening. Safety pins of several sizes, all looped to the largest. Some copper rivets. An empty toothpaste tube that will serve as emergency solder when used with the pitch of a handy evergreen tree for flux.

Finally, I have a small sewing roll that can be shifted to a pocket when I'm traveling too light for the entire repair kit. This contains strong thread, wax for further strengthening it, assorted needles, and a couple of cards that I've wound with darning wool for sock repair. There are only several buttons, as they can be easily improvised from leather, bone, or wood.

SOMETHING ALWAYS TO CARRY

The following GOLD/SILVER WEIGHT CONVERSION TABLE, copyrighted 1978 by G. M. Miller, was prepared by the *National Prospector's Gazette* of Ames, Nebraska 68621, and is reprinted with the permission of Exanimo Establishment in Fremont, Nebraska 68025.

To find conversion values, find the basic weight in the left-hand column and follow this line until it intersects with the desired weight. For example, if you desire to determine how many "ounces Troy" there are in a "pound Troy," locate POUND TROY in the left-hand column and follow it across until you intersect with OUNCE TROY and you will find 12.0, which is the correct number of ounces Troy in one pound Troy. Then, if you want to know how many ounces there are in 2½ pounds Troy, multiply 12.0 by 2½ and arrive at a correct figure of 30 ounces Troy. Another valuable way to use this table is for comparative purposes: for comparing avoirdupois against Troy, for example. If you want to compare the relative actual weight of a pound Troy against an avoirdupois pound, follow the POUND AV line across the POUND TROY column and you can determine that a pound avoirdupois is equal to 1.21107 pounds Troy. Using the same method, you will find that an ounce avoirdupois is equal to 0.9114883 ounce Troy. Anyone who buys or sells gold or silver will find hundreds of valuable applications for this table.

	GRAIN	GRAM	DWT TROY	OZ TROY	LB TROY	OZ AV	LB AV	CARAT
GRAIN	1.0	0.06479	0.041667	0.0020833	0.00017	0.0022887	0.0001428	0.3240
GRAM	15.4324	1.0	0.06479	0.03215	0.0027	0.03527	0.002205	5.0
DWT TROY	24.0	1.5517	1.0	0.05	0.00416	0.0548571	0.0034285	7.7755
OUNCE TROY	480.0	31.10346	20.0	1.0	0.0833	1.09714	0.06857	155.51
POUND TROY	5780.0	373.241	240.0	12.0	1.0	13.1657	0.82286	1866.12
OUNCE AV	437.0	28.3495	18.2297	0.9114883	0.07594	1.0	0.0625	141.75
POUND AV	7000.0	453.592	291.667	14.5833	1.21107	16.0	1.0	2267.96
CARAT	3.168	0.20	0.03215	0.0064304	0.000536	0.007055	0.000441	1.0

Abbreviations: AV = Avoirdupois, DWT = Pennyweight, LB = Pound, OZ = Ounce

Chapter Fourteen

SOURDOUGH AND POWDERED EGGS

EXCEPT FOR A preferably large boiling utensil, which will be practically a necessity if you plan to live to any reasonable extent off the country, you can get along without much of a cooking outfit when you're prospecting close to civilization. One of the old surplus frypans will do a lot of jobs although, actually, it is heavier than necessary. Yet the high bowl-like sides make it admirable even for stews. If you'll cover sourdough bread or a roast with the platelike lid, the whole thing can be buried in hot coals and ashes like a miniature Dutch oven. If you choose to carry one of the old surplus canteens as well, it will be just about as easy to include the cup which fits over the end and can be used in numerous ways.

Handiest of all in the culinary department, and what you'll need in the bush, is one of the small nested sets that are available at sporting goods stores and through some of the large catalog-issuing firms. Get the best obtainable. Even this will be far more functional if the cups and preferably the plates as well are made of stainless steel rather than of the more fragile, all too ardent aluminum. A steel frypan with a folding handle is a wise choice as well.

LIGHTWEIGHT RATIONS

For the long pull, you'll find that fat, in calories the most concentrated of foods, is the hardest to come by when you're living to some extent off the country. Butter, margarine, bacon drippings, and lard for example boast more than double the calories, ounce for ounce, than such a staple as sugar and nearly three times as much as honey. For limited rations for wilderness stints of undetermined duration you may determine, therefore, to pack along a preponderance of edible fats with the idea of partly completing your diet from natural sources.

For the shorter haul, you may care to include some of the compact, tasty, and nutritious rations now especially manufactured for campers as a whole and for exploration teams and other scientific adventurers such as prospectors in particular.

The source of such preassembled meals and other dehydrated camp fare with which I am most familiar is Chuck Wagon Foods, Micro Drive, Woburn, Massachusetts 01801. Also, more and more lightweight, dry food preparations are available at competitive prices in the supermarkets. These, in many instances are suitable when repacked more compactly.

PACKING

Dry foods such as flour, cereal, beans, salt, and sugar can be packed in small waterproof sacks which are available in a variety of types and sizes from most camp outfitters. You can make them, too. Each should be plainly labeled. Repackage dry foods whenever this can be done advantageously, cutting out and enclosing any special directions. Unless you've plenty of room, foods such as corn flakes should be compressed into as small a space as possible.

Dried meats may be wrapped in wax paper or aluminum foil. Lard, margarine, and the like travel well in tightly closed tins. Plastic flasks and bottles made for carrying most liquids are safer and lighter than glass for syrups, oils, and such, but not for most extracts. Powdered eggs and milk will keep better in snugly closed receptacles. Beverages in powdered form should also be kept tightly closed.

CHEESE

Cheese is one of the most versatile and delectable of camp foods. It may be relished in its natural state or added to everything from soups and salads to sauces to make all sorts of delicious combinations. A sharp, aged cheddar keeps well, as does edam and gouda. Provalone is probably the best choice in high temperatures.

If heat makes your cheese rubbery, a solution is to wrap it well and revive it in a cool stream. If you're going to spend a month or more away from civilization, sew one-week portions snugly in cheesecloth and immerse them in melted wax. You can harmlessly keep mold off cheese to a large extent by wiping the cheese in a clean cloth soaked either in baking soda solution or in vinegar. The same thing goes for sliced bacon.

DRY MILK

Powdered milk is especially handy in cold weather if only because the quality of evaporated milk is impaired by freezing which, for that matter, can cause it to spoil entirely by bursting the can. Besides, evaporated milk is still ¾ water. Condensed milk is ¼ water and nearly ½ sugar. Depending on the product, one pound of whole milk makes one gallon of liquid whole milk.

Dried skim milk has all the nourishment of fresh skim milk. It has the calcium, phosphorous, iron and other minerals, the B vitamins, natural sugar, and the protein that makes liquid skim milk such an important food. Powdered whole milk has all these, plus the fat and vitamin A found in the cream of whole milk. Adding two teaspoons of butter or margarine to a cup of reconstituted skim milk will make this equal in food value to a cup of whole milk.

POWDERED EGGS

An egg is 11% waste unless you are going to bake the shells and then pulverize them, as some do to increase the calcium content of their dogs' feed. Seventy-four percent of the remaining white and yolk is water. Yet white dried egg has virtually the same food value, includes no waste, and is only a tiny proportion water.

The flavor of egg powder cooked by itself is not like that of fresh eggs. Most of us in the contiguous United States are accustomed to the latter. Our natural taste reaction, therefore, is that the former is inferior. With different eating habits, as many have witnessed in Europe, this taste prejudice also works the other way around.

In any event, scrambled eggs prepared from the powder come to taste mighty good back of beyond. If you haven't prepared these before, dissolve powdered eggs and milk in lukewarm water to make the proportions of those fresh products you would ordinarily use. Add salt, pepper, and any other seasoning, together with a chunk of butter or or margarine. A little flour may be stirred in for thickening. Scrambling all this with ham or bacon gives the dish added flavor.

SOURDOUGH BREAD

Sourdough bread is particularly designed to solve the problems of the ofttimes unskilled wilderness cook. Considerable folklore has sprung up around this pioneer staple which, early proving its ability to rise under just about any condition short of freezing, gave veteran northerners their names of Sourdoughs. You hear tales of sourdough that has been kept going ever since Alaskan and Klondike gold rush days near the turn of the century. Many of such accounts are completely true.

For the taste of real sourdough bread, you can get a dollar packet of Bradford Angier Sourdough Starter, plus a pamphlet of recipes, from Chuck Wagon Foods, Micro Drive, Woburn, Massachusetts 01801. Or start your own primitive sourdough starter by mixing a cup apiece of plain flour and water in a scalded jar, covering it loosely, and placing it in a warm place to sour. If the first results are not satisfactory, and it all depends on what wild yeasts you capture from the air, try again with a new mixture. Once you have your starter, that part of the process is finished. You have commenced growing your own yeast.

To make sourdough bread, take your starter. Add enough flour and lukewarm water to make about three cups of sponge. Let this stand in a warm place overnight, or at a minimum from six to eight hours, whereupon it should be bubbling and emitting an agreeable, yeasty odor.

Take out, in this instance, two cups of sponge. Place the remainder aside in a well-washed and scalded glass or pottery container. Keep in a cool spot. This is your next starter. No matter what the recipe, at this stage always keep out a cup of the basic sourdough.

To these two cups of sponge add 4 cups flour, 2 tablespoons sugar, 1 teaspoon salt, and 2 tablespoons shortening.

Mix, the flour, sugar, and salt. Make a depression in the center of these dry ingredients. Melt the shortening if it is not already liquid. Blend it and the sponge in the hollow. Then mix everything together. A soft dough should result. If necessary, add either flour or fluid. The latter may be milk or water. Knead for three or four minutes on a clean, floured surface.

"Keep attacking," I can still hear an old prospector cautioning, eyes blinking amiably behind thick-lensed spectacles. "Don't gentle it. That's where most cheechakos made their mistake. Too much pushing and pressing lets the gas escape that is needed to raise the stuff. Just bang the dough together in a hurry, cut off loaves to fit your greased pans, and put them in a warm place to raise."

The dough, once it has plumped out to double size, is often most handily cooked in a reflector oven for about an hour in direct campfire heat, ideally in highest heat the first dozen minutes. Or leave it in your Dutch oven, buried under that morning's embers, before heading out of camp for the day.

Baking should redouble the size of the loaves. When the bread seems crisply brown, test by jabbing in a straw. If the bread is done, the straw will come out dry and clean. Or with a little more experience listen for the hollow sound the finished loaves will give when thumped on top. Remove from the oven, turn out on a rack or towel, and butter the tops.

Sourdough bread is substantial in comparison with the usual air-filled baker loaf. It keeps moist for a satisfyingly long time. When the bread is made according to the preceding suggestions, the flavor is unusually excellent, being especially nutty when slices are toasted. If your family likes real tastry crust, bake the bread in long slim loaves to capitalize on this outstanding characteristic.

FRYING PAN BREAD

This is the famous bannock of the open places. The basic recipe for one hungry prospector follows. If you want more, just increase the ingredients proportionately.

> 1 cup flour
> 1 teaspoon double-action baking powder
> ½ teaspoon salt.

Mix these dry, taking all the time you need to do this throughly. Have the hands floured and everything ready to go before you add liquid. If you are going to use the traditional frypan, make sure it is warm and greased.

Working quickly from now on, stir in enough cold water to make a firm dough. Shape this, with as little handling as possible, into a cake about an inch thick. If you like crust, leave a doughnut-like hole in the center. Dust the loaf lightly with flour, so it will handle more easily.

Lay the bannock in the warm frypan. Hold it over the heat until a bottom crust forms, rotating the pan a little so the loaf will shift and not become stuck.

Once the dough has hardened enough to hold together, you can turn the bannock over. This, if you've practiced a bit and have the confidence to flip strongly enough, can be easily accomplished with a slight swing of the arm and snap of the wrist. Or you can use a spatula, supporting the loaf long enough to invert the frypan over it and then turning everything together.

With a campfire, however, it is often easier at this stage just to prop the frypan at a steep angle so that the bannock will get direct heat on top. When crust has formed all around, you may if you wish to, turn the bannock over and around a few times while it is cooking to an appetizing brown.

When is the bannock done? After you've been cooking them awhile, you will be able to tap one and gage this by the hollowness of the sound. Meanwhile, test by shoving in a straw or sliver. If any dough adheres, the loaf needs more heat. Cooking can be accomplished in about 15 minutes. If you have other duties around camp, twice that time a bit further from the heat will allow the bannock to cook more evenly.

Bannock, in any event, never tastes better than when devoured piping hot around a campfire. It should then be broken apart, never cut. A cold bannock sliced in half, however, and made into a man-size sandwich with plenty of meat or other filler in between is the best lunch ever.

THE CALORIE STORY

You can, if weight and space are at extreme premium, use a calorie chart as a basis for figuring how to go about packing the most nourishment with the least trouble. Briefly, you're burning up a certain amount of energy every second. Energy not supplied directly by a sufficiency of food is taken from the body's carbohydrates, fats, and proteins.

Even when you're sleeping relaxed in the most comfortable of eiderdowns, your system is consuming heat units, or calories, at the rate of approximately 10 calories a day per pound of body weight. In other words, if you weigh 160 pounds, the least number of calories you'll use each day is 1,600. These basic requirements diminish but slightly, as a matter of fact, even when an individual is starving.

The more you move around and the more energy you expend in keeping warm, the more calories you use. Even lying in your sleeping bag and reading will increase your basic caloric needs about 25%. The city man who gets very little exercise consumes on the average 50% above his minimum requirements. To maintain his weight, therefore, such a 160-pound individual requires about 2,400 calories daily.

It is reasonable, both from these scientific facts and from personal experience, to generalize that a healthy and fit man enjoying a robust outdoor life can require 20 calories of food a day per pound of body weight—and perhaps more, depending on his activity and the climate. Cold weather, for example, compels the system to put out more and more heat to keep itself warm. The same 160-pound city man prospecting in the north woods can very easily take in 3,200 or 4,000 calories a day, and more, and still trim down lean and hard.

PROVISIONING FOR PROSPECTING

With appetites sharpened by the sort of robust outdoor living for which man was bred, meals afield can be just as nourishing and tasty as those in town, and maybe more so—when you take foods that keep well, cook quickly, and are easy to carry. There is no good reason for suggesting any particular grub lists or daily menus, for what suits one will not always satisfy another. You'll do best to bring what you personally like and what you'll find easiest to prepare.

Experimentation is the best way to find out how much of each item you'll need to round out a satisfactory meal. If you want oatmeal porridge every morning, for example, find out just how many rolled oats are needed to make the breakfast you will likely eat in the field. Just as a suggestion, take at least double the amount of sugar and sweets you would use at home, for your desire for them will be out of all proportion to that in the city.

Here's a yardstick you may find valuable. General speaking, the total weight of reasonably water-free foods you will want to eat should not be less than 2¼ pounds per man per day. This does not include fresh vegetables and fruits. For the purposes of figuring, consult the following table to ascertain the weight relationship of these to their dehydrated equivalents.

The following chart may be used for scientifically planning a light, compact grubstake made up largely of high-energy rations.

The nutrient values, based on official researches of two governments with standard United States and Canadian foods, will vary somewhat in different localities. Dehydrated products will naturally differ to an even broader extent, depending not only on the original raw products but also on processing methods. Slight seasonal variations in food content have been ignored, being unimportant to the aspects here considered.

Calories	One-Pound Portion	Outfitting Data
2709	Almonds, shelled, dried	1 cup shelled - 5⅓ oz.
1680	Apples, dried	1 lb. dried - 8 lbs. fresh
1634	Apricots, dried	1 lb. dry - 5½ lb. fresh
1047	Bacon, back	3 slices, 2½″ diam. x ¼″ - 3½ oz.
2855	Bacon, side	1 lb. - 20 to 24 slices 2½ to 3 slices - 2 oz.
1219	Banana, dried	3½ oz. dried - about 1 lb. fresh
1536	Barley, brown, whole	2 tbsp. dry - 1 oz.
1525	Beans, dried, kidney	1 lb - 2⅔ cups 1 lb - 7 cups cooked
1512	Beans, Lima	1 lb. - 2⅓ cups 1 lb. - 6½ cups cooked
1535	Beans, Navy	1 lb. - 2⅓ cups 1 lb. - 6 cups cooked
977	Beef, corned, canned	3 slices 3″ x 2½″ x ¼″ - 3½ oz. 16 slices to 1 lb.
922	Beef, dried or chipped	2 thin slices - 1 oz.
1004	Bologna	1 slice - 4½″ diam. x ⅛″ - 1 oz.
3248	Butter	1 lb. - 2 cups
1587	Cabbage, dehydrated	1 lb. serves 50 1 serving - ⅓ oz.
1641	Carrots, dehydrated	1 lb. serves 25 1 serving raw - 4 oz. cooked
2619	Cashews	4 to 5 nuts - ½ oz.
1804	Cheese, cheddar	1 lb. cheese grated - 4 cups
1676	Cheese, cheddar processed	
433	Cheese, cottage	1 lb. - 2 cups, serves 8 1 serving, ¼ cup - 2 oz.
1684	Cheese, cream	2 tablespooons - 1 oz.
1679	Cheese, Swiss	1 slice, 4½″ x 3½″ x ⅛″ - 1 oz.
905	Chicken, canned, boned	½ cup - 3½ oz.
2273	Chocolate, bitter	1 lb. melted - 2 cups

Calories	One-Pound Portion	Outfitting Data
2282	Chocolate, milk, plain	
2413	Chocolate, milk, with almonds	
2403	Chocolate, bittersweet	
2136	Chocolate, sweetened, plain	
1329	Cocoa, dry	1 lb. - 4 cups
1316	Coffee, roasted	1 lb. - 5½ cups finely ground, makes 50 cups. Contains, in solid state, 1316 calories.
1649	Corn meal, yellow	3 cups weigh 1 lb.
4013	Corn oil	1 lb. - 2 cups
1642	Cornstarch	1 lb. - 3½ cups (stirred)
4013	Cotton seed oil	1 lb. - 2 cups
1287	Dates, dried, pitted	1 lb. pitted and cut - 2½ cups
655	Eggs, fresh, whole	1 doz. extra large - 27 oz. up 1 doz. large - at least 24 oz. 1 doz. medium - 21 to 24 oz.
2688	Egg, dried, whole	¼ cup powder & 1½ cups water - 1 doz. fresh eggs
1530	Farina, dark	3 tbsp. dry - 1 oz. yield ¾ cup cooked
1677	Farina, light	1 lb. - approximately 2⅔ cups dry
357	Figs, fresh, raw	2 medium - 4 oz.
514	Figs, canned in syrup	½ cup weighs 3½ oz.
1223	Figs, dried	3 cups (44 figs) - 1 lb.
2838	Filberts, shelled	1 cup - 4¾ oz.
1643	Flour, buckwheat, light	1 cup - 4¼ oz.
1574	Flour, dark	1 cup - 4¼ oz.
1659	Flour, rye, light	1 lb. rye flour - about 4½ cups 1 lb. sifted - 5⅔ cups
1442	Flour, rye, dark	
1632	Flour, wheat	All-purpose flour - 4 cups per lb. sifted Cake flour - 4¾ cups per lb. sifted Pastry flour - 4¾ cups per lb. sifted
1586	Flour, self-rising	4 cups per lb. sifted
1510	Flour, whole	Whole wheat flour stirred - 3¾ cups per lb.
317	Fruit cocktail, canned	No. 2 can - 1 lb.
1739	Gelatin, dessert powder	2½ cups per lb. 1 oz. pkg. makes 4 to 6 servings
1643	Hominy, grits	3 cups per lb. 3 tbsp. raw - ⅔ cup cooked

Calories	One-Pound Portion	Outfitting Data
1400	Honey	1 lb. - 1⅓ cups
1262	Jam, assorted	3 level tbsp. - 2 oz.
4091	Lard	2 cups per lb. 1 oz. measures 2 tbsp.
1530	Lentils, dry	2⅓ cups per lb. 2½ tbsp. dry - 1 oz. - yields ½ cup cooked
1928	Liverwurst	1 slice 3" diam, ¼" thick - 1 oz.
1723	Macaroni	1 lb. 1" pieces - 4 cups 1 lb. cooked 12 cups - weighs 4 lbs.
624	Milk, evaporated	1 lb. tin & equal water - 1½ pints fresh milk
2231	Milk, powdered, whole	1 lb - 3½ cups 4 tbsp. level & 1 cup water - 1 cup fresh milk
1642	Milk, powdered, skim	⅓ cup 7¾ cup water - 1 cup fresh skim milk 3.2 oz. makes 1 qt.
1142	Molasses	1 cup weighs 11 oz.
107	Mushrooms, fresh, raw	4 large or 10 small - 3½ oz.
1728	Noodles, containing egg	1" pieces - 6 cups to 1 lb. 1 lb. yields 11 cups cooked
1794	Oats, meal or rolled	1 lb. - 5⅔ cups ⅓ cup makes 1 cup porridge
3266	Oleomargarine	1 tbsp. - ½ oz.
4013	Olive oil	1 lb. - 2 cups
308	Peaches, canned in syrup	2 halves & 3 tbsp. juice - 4 oz.
1634	Peaches, dried	1 lb. dried - 5½ lbs. fresh
2613	Peanut butter	1 lb. - 2 cups
1219	Pears, dried	1 lb. dried - 5½ lbs. fresh
193	Peas, fresh	2.2 lbs. whole - 1 lb. shelled (3 cups)
1540	Peas, dried, green	2 tbsp. dry - 1 oz. yields ½ cup cooked
1562	Peas, split	2¼ cups - 1 lb.
3159	Pecans, shelled	1 lb. in shell yields ⅓ lb. meats
3410	Pork, salt, fat, with rind	2 slices 4" x 2" x ⅜" - 3½ oz.
318	Potatoes, fresh	1 lb. as purchased - 3 to 4 servings
1620	Potatoes, dehydrated	1 serving - 1 oz. dry - 4 oz. reconstituted
1034	Prunes, dried, with pits	Sizes - large 20 to 40 per lb., medium 40 to 60 per lb., small 60 to 100 per lb.

Calories	One-Pound Portion	Outfitting Data
1725	Prunes, dried, pitted	1 lb. cooked with 2 qts. water gives 2½ qts.
1217	Raisins, dried	Seeded, 3¼ cups - 1 lb. Seedless, whole 2¾ cups - 1 lb.
1648	Rice, brown	2 tbsp. dry - 1 oz. yields ½ cup cooked
1629	Rice, white	1 lb. 2⅛ cups, 7 cups when cooked
1682	Rice, wild	1 lb. - 3 cups 1 oz. - 3 tbsp. - 1 serving
1787	Salad dressing, French	2 tbsp. - 1 oz.
3211	Salad dressing, mayonnaise	2 tbsp. - 1 oz.
1531	Sardines in oil	15 sardines 3″ long - 5 oz.
784	Sardines in tomato sauce	
1817	Sausage, salami in casing	1 slice 4½″ diam., ⅛″ thick - 1 oz.
1164	Sausage, weiners, raw	7 to 9 per lb.
4010	Shortening, vegetable, Crisco, Spry, etc.	1 lb. - 2¼ cups
1719	Spaghetti	1 lb. broken - 4¾ cups
3437	Suet	1 lb. ground suet - 3½ cups
1676	Sugar, brown	2 cups (firmly packed) - 1 lb.
1747	Sugar, granulated, white	1 lb. - 2¼ cups
1747	Sugar, icing	1 lb. - 3½ cups
1747	Sugar, loaf	Flat tablets, 100 to 1 lb.
1580	Sugar, maple	1 piece 1″ x 1¼″ x ½″ - ½ oz.
1299	Syrups, corn	1⅓ cups per lb.
1123	Syrups, maple	1½ cups per lb.
1633	Tapioca, dry, pearl	2¾ cups raw - 7½ cups cooked
	Tea	1 lb. - 6 cups dry makes 200 to 300 cups
2969	Walnuts, shelled	1 lb. in shell - ⅓ lb. meats 1 lb. halves - 4½ cups
1639	Wheat, germ	1 tbsp. - ⅙ oz.
1544	Whole wheat, dry	⅓ cup dry - 1 oz. - ¾ cup cooked

INDEX